love
for
grown
-ups

love
= for =
grown
-ups

The Garter Brides'
Guide to Marrying for Life
When You've Already Got a Life

Ann Blumenthal Jacobs
Patricia Ryan Lampl
Tish Rabe

with Toni Sciarra Poynter

Love for Grown-ups

ISBN-13: 978-0-373-89236-5

Library of Congress Cataloging-in-Publication Data
Jacobs, Ann Blumenthal.
Love for grown-ups : the garter brides™ guide to marrying for life when you've already got a life
Ann Blumenthal Jacobs, Patricia Ryan Lampl and Tish Rabe.
p. cm.
ISBN 978-0-373-89236-5 (pbk.)
1. Man-woman relationships. 2. Dating (Social customs). 3. Marriage. 4. Single women--Psychology. 5. Middle-aged women--Psychology. 6. Older women--Psychology. I. Title.
HQ801 .J229 2011
646.7—dc22
2010035363

www.Harlequin.com

Printed in U.S.A.

To Irv, who makes all my dreams come true. —Ann

To Mark, Sophie, Melissa and Stephen, my heart's desire. —Pat

To John, whose love and complete faith in me gives me wings. —Tish

ACKNOWLEDGMENTS

There are so many people we wish to thank for helping us with this book, but it all happened because of our wonderful agent, Garter Bride Chris Tomasino. For her talent, determination, dedication and encouragement throughout the entire process, she has our eternal gratitude.

Working with three authors could only have been handled so expertly by Toni Sciarra Poynter. Her skill, thoughtful organization and unfailing sense of humor have been astonishing. We are truly grateful. We couldn't have done it without her! We always felt Harlequin was the right place for us and fortunately our editor, Deborah Brody, did, too. Her help and support are truly appreciated.

Thanks to all our family and friends, who rooted for us the whole way. For their generosity of spirit, time and talent we want to thank Cynthia Finn Barry, Gloria Bremer, John Caffrey, Rollene Saal Forma, Lynn Goldberg, Mike Levesque, Mike Levesque Jr., Tim Meola, Brenda Philip, Melody Rabe, Johnny Rabe, Kevin Ryan, Lisa Schultz, Dr. Leigh Simone, Tina Beana Strasberg, Bonnie Stylides, Bob Watson and Claire McKean, who believed in our book from the beginning.

We would also like to thank those who gave us support in unique and important ways: Stephen Donovan, Edward Nunes, Eda Rak, Angela Seracini and Peter Zimmerman.

And a special thank you to all the Garter Brides who shared their stories and wisdom. Your enthusiasm and sharing of your happy lives were true gifts and you've become our friends and sisters.

And finally, most important of all, our thanks to the very first Garter Bride, Nina Weber Worth, who started the tradition.

CONTENTS

CONTENTS

INTRODUCTION
How a Little Garter Led to a Lot of Love
The Story of the Garter Brides

It's a luscious experience, falling in love as a grown-up. You're wise to the relationship hazards that used to snag you, you know what's important in a partner and won't settle for anything less and you're ready to meet a man as an equal on every level, including horizontally!

And those are all good things.

We wrote this book just for you.

If you're single and wondering whether you'll ever find someone to love, if you're dating a special guy and not sure whether you should take your relationship to the next level or if you're on the fence about going after grown-up love with all the hope and passion in your heart, the Garter Brides say, "A thousand times yes!" We know, because we did it—and we're on a mission to show other women how.

Love for Grown-ups is a relationship book full of field-tested advice from us and from other women who found lasting love and happiness after our thirty-fifth birthdays had come . . . and gone. We're not psychologists or relationship experts, but honors graduates of the School of Relationship Hard Knocks: we've forged happy, successful, sexy, fun, grown-up marriages not when the storybooks predict, but when we and our husbands had histories, careers, furniture, sometimes children, ex-spouses and all kinds of responsibilities.

We knew there were lots of other women out there who had done what we did. We've sought them out, tapped into their insights about what works and what doesn't and want to share the tried-and-true wisdom of this special sisterhood with you.

What can we tell you about grown-up love? Between us and the many women we've interviewed, quite a lot. We won't insult your intelligence with babble about getting in touch with your inner beauty. Let's talk turkey: you're a hot babe with a busy life you'd love to share, a cozy bed into which you'd welcome a good man for some great sex and great fun, and a well-oiled BS detector you didn't possess in your twenties. You're mature enough to handle grown-up love, to move forward without looking back and to appreciate how great a gift that is.

Like you, we took some extra time to find our own true loves—and it was well worth the wait. But marrying later in life isn't as simple as finding Mr. Right, getting married and having a family. We know a lot of grown-up women whose relationships failed because they didn't know how to handle some of the situations they faced. We want to make sure that doesn't happen to you.

Who Are the Garter Brides (GBs)?

It all started, as many great adventures do, with girlfriends having dinner (i.e., drinks). Nina, Ann and Pat were business colleagues and longtime friends, all over the age of thirty-five. All had successful careers and were going on dates (approximately 9,000 of those by Pat alone, according to her), but none of them thought she'd get married.

But . . .

Six months later, Nina got married. Six months after that, Ann got married. Six months after *that,* Pat got married.

Nina said, "At my age you wear a garter, but you don't throw it." She slipped it off and gave it to Ann, who wore it at her wedding. Ann then gave it to Pat, who wore it at her wedding. They named themselves the Garter Brides—and a new tradition was born!

Today, this good-luck garter has been worn by girlfriends ranging in age from thirty-eight to fifty-seven, and it has traveled—in a FedEx box—all over the United States and even to that city of ultimate newlywed bliss, Venice!

Everyone who's heard about the Garter Brides has been captivated by the story of how this little scrap of lingerie was part of so many happy endings—or shall we say beginnings? One of the many women who loved hearing the Garter Brides' story was Tish Rabe, because she kept on believing in grown-up love when she found her own happy beginning: she married for the first time at thirty-six—to a man she'd known since high school! She encouraged Ann and Pat to share their stories, and thus the idea for *Love for Grown-ups* came to be.

From a Tiny Garter, a Sisterhood Grows

All of the Garter Brides have been questioned repeatedly about how they met their husbands and made new lives with the men they loved. How is a mature marriage different from when you get married in your twenties? Keep reading!

Where dating books leave off (although we talk about dating, too), the Garter Brides' book continues. We know that a grown-up woman's wedding is just the beginning of a rich, rewarding life—one she probably couldn't have handled when she was twenty-five. (As one woman we know says, "Thank God I met my mother-in-law when I was thirty-five—at twenty-two, she would have eaten me alive!")

We're writing this book on the best authority: our own life experiences and those of women we've interviewed around the world, from ages thirty-seven to eighty, who have applied their grown-up life experiences to forge happy, sex-filled marriages in all types of circumstances. We are producers, lawyers, actresses, teachers, masseuses, psychologists, yoga teachers, agents, writers, fashionistas, art critics, financial advisers, nurses, real estate brokers and even a dancer of the bump-and-grind variety!

Some of us are first-timers at marriage; for some it's husband number two and for others it's husband number three. Some became stepmoms, first-time moms or stepgrandmoms and a number of the brides adopted children. We met our true loves in all sorts of ways—blind dates, parties, online dating, the commuter train, even while taking flying lessons. Our dream weddings ran the gamut from ultra-glam to super-casual; our households are filled with everything from antiques to running toddlers to crazy Jack Russell terriers. And we have great "here's how I did it" stories to share about moving in together, becoming a stepfamily, navigating finances and the art of joining two full and complex lives.

As a result, we have a unique handle on what it takes to make grown-up relationships work. We and our fellow brides are living proof that finding the right guy and making a wonderful marriage is possible at any stage of life. We've learned a lot, we're still learning (as Pat says, one great thing about being married is that there are plenty of do-over opportunities) and we're still laughing. It's this mix of real-life lessons and strategies for staying flexible and enjoying the humor along the way that we want to share with other grown-up brides and brides-to-be.

We know how woman-to-woman support—being able to turn to others who've been there—helped our own loves flourish. Grown-up love is both wonderful and complicated. Sometimes it may feel lonely when you're dealing with relationship challenges. What we've learned from connecting with so many women is that you are never alone.

We've laughed and cried together as we've shared experiences and insights. We've become more convinced than ever of the importance of our mission to gather and share women's wisdom about this unique time in life. We've formed a sisterhood of women—all Garter Brides— who want to encourage all women to take a chance on grown-up love and have the life they always dreamed of.

What to Expect from This Book

If you're still looking for that special someone, we'll show you how to take a fresh approach to dating, stay open to the promise of grown-up love and have fun—whether the next date is Mr. Right or Mr. What-Was-I-Thinking?

If you've found the terrific guy you deserve, we'll share ideas for developing your relationship and combining two busy lives.

Grown-up love raises a lot of questions: Are one or both of you divorced or widowed? Are exes in the picture—and just how pretty is that picture? What's the best way to welcome stepchildren and build these new relationships? Speaking of children, does anyone hear a biological clock ticking? What's important to know about living together before getting married—and should the new "we" live in your place or his? Who makes the move if it's a long-distance relationship? How should grown-up finances be handled?

To help you quickly pick up the take-home info, each chapter is organized by the key questions women commonly ask (or should). We reveal the issues and answers women need to keep in mind as they find true love and build a life together. We flesh out our ideas with anecdotes and examples from our experiences and those of other grown-up brides, all served with a double scoop of Garter Bride attitude. We've also created a website (www.thegarterbrides.com) where we offer additional up-to-the-minute tips and advice on real-life situations, and you can visit us on Facebook and Twitter. On our site you'll get to meet other Garter Brides who share their stories and you can share yours. We want to get to know you, too! We also invite you to ask us questions so we can help you in creating a new life with the man you love.

So get ready to meet the Garter Brides because for every woman seeking the love of her life or embarking on a special relationship, we are here to bring hope, help and hilarity.

Meet the GBs

Before we launch into our advice, you should get to know us better. The first things you need to know about us are that (1) we laugh a lot—especially at ourselves—and (2) although we have opinions about everything, we're far from perfect. Our lives are full of the usual stuff: work complications; kid crises; pesky relatives; missed deadlines; messy drawers; unruly hair; pounds gained, lost and regained; purchases we regret; girlfriends we can't live without.

One thing we all also have—which both delights and humbles us—is husbands who absolutely adore us, regardless of the aforementioned usual stuff. The wonder of being adored by a man for everything we are—and despite everything we aren't—is our wish for you, and one of our reasons for writing this book. You'll learn more about us throughout the book, but to get started, here's a snapshot of each of us.

GARTER BRIDE RAP SHEET: PAT LAMPL

Name: Patricia Mary Agnes Ryan Lampl

Occupation: Magazine columnist, author and award-winning television producer; with Ann Jacobs, a partner in On the Aisle Productions, a media consulting company

Married to: Mark Lampl

Kids: Two stepchildren; one child with Mark; two step-grandchildren

Most quotable line: "When I went shopping for my wedding dress as a first-time bride at thirty-nine, three salespeople asked me if this was my second marriage. I finally regained my sense of humor and told them that I'd waited so long I skipped the first and went right to the second! Who cared what number it was?"

Most bizarre Garter Bride moment: Becoming a mother and a stepgrandmother in the same year!

Favorite thing about being married to Mark: Laughing together until our faces hurt.

Favorite grown-up bride coping strategy: Don't lose sight of the big picture. And get caller ID.

Greatest thing about being a Garter Bride: When we go out, it's still a dream date!

The thing you need to know about Mark is that he's a doer. He pursues possibilities most people wouldn't even consider. And because he's ever hopeful, he's always prepared. For example, he travels a lot for work and he automatically rents a car in the city he's visiting, because you never know if you might need wheels to follow up on a business lead in a nearby town.

So when he called a work colleague for a date only to find that she'd just gotten engaged the week before, he naturally asked, "Do you know anyone else?"

For Mark it was the equivalent, in dating terms, of prospecting for business the next town over. Never get off the phone without a referral, right?

It so happened that this woman worked with a dear college friend of mine, and the three of us had gone out for chick dinners together. "What about Pat?" the newly betrothed chick asked. "No way!" said my college friend. "They have nothing in common." But she, too, liked Mark, so they figured what the heck.

So here was their pitch: "There's this nice guy named Mark. He's divorced, has two kids, comes up here to the New York office pretty frequently but lives in Atlanta—yeah, Atlanta—but he's a really nice guy."

"Do you hate me?" I said. "I need a guy like this like I need a bigger rear end."

I'd been on 9,000 blind dates. No way was a guy who lived 800 miles away going to be blind date number 9,001. Talk about unavailability. On which I was an expert, by the way. I was actually dating— I use the term as loosely as he did—a gorgeous, sexy engineer from Massachusetts who was working on a project in New York. He'd call at the last minute (never, of course, when I expected) and blow into town for a whirlwind good time, then disappear again, leaving me to wait by the phone for the next wave of inordinate, inappropriate and inconsistent attention. It was heaven, if you liked the thrill of never knowing which end was up. As it seemed I did.

"Look, I really like this guy," my college friend pleaded. "For God's sake, have a glass of wine with him when he's in New York. You don't have to marry him." (How often have we all heard that?)

Mark and I talked on the phone two or three times before we met. My friends were right: he was nice. On his next trip to New York, we planned to go out for dinner. Clearly he knew nothing about the New York dating scene. So when he came to pick me up straight from the airport with a huge suitcase and said, "I'll just leave this here," he was oblivious to my deer-in-the-headlights expression.

I'd had a lot of horrible blind dates, but none so far had made headlines in the *New York Post*. Was I, after a glass of mediocre wine and a plate of ravioli, going to experience my very own fifteen minutes of infamy? "Uh, why don't you take it to the restaurant?" I asked. "No, it's too heavy. I'll just leave it here and come back," he said. So we left, with me trying to remember if I'd called any girlfriends to say I was going on a date that night.

Our dinner stretched to three hours. We discovered we're both travel nuts, and we talked up a storm. Afterward, he picked up his bag at my apartment and left. My life had been spared. What I didn't realize then was that it had been changed. I thought he was cute, but I felt no fireworks. For that, remember, I had Mr. Unavailable.

Did I mention I was also dating a personal trainer? It was one of the few times in my dating life that I had a lot going on. Maybe that's why it worked between Mark and me. I wasn't anxious over the outcome—I was just me being me. Besides which, if I started to take this guy seriously, he might leave me. Weirdly enough, it just felt safer to keep having unpredictable, hot dates with Mr. Unavailable, because that way I would be either (1) having so much fun or (2) so busy obsessing about whether he'd call that I didn't have to face that there was no real future there.

So began a slow, rather old-fashioned courtship by phone and occasional face-to-face meetings. Mark and I got to know each other. What a concept.

One evening I was walking home through Central Park after a tough day at work, worrying about some political complication that was going on there. I remembered Mark had said he was going to call at seven-thirty—just ten minutes away. *I've got to ask Mark about this,* I thought.

He called. I talked. He listened. He suggested ways to handle the situation. His advice was great. I hung up the phone, and suddenly the revelation was right there in front of me: *Wow. He's the go-to guy. He said he was going to call at seven-thirty. And he did. Then he listened to me. And then he helped me. I really liked that. Maybe loving somebody isn't worrying about what's going on with him and constantly wondering whether he's going to call and want to see you. Maybe it's not about anxiety. Maybe it's about safety. Could I have called Mr. Unavailable with a problem? I don't think so, because that wouldn't have been "fun," now, would it?*

I decided right then to be in a relationship, *this* relationship. I decided to give this guy a shot. It didn't really change the way we interacted that much, but it became different for me because *I* was different. I was falling in love.

You'll learn in later chapters about how we resolved the long-distance thing, about how we worked out a big issue for many grown-up couples—having a child—and about the proposal in Paris. (Hint: his big romantic pop-the-question plans went down the toilet—twice!) Suffice it to say that our wedding cake had a little Eiffel Tower on top. Now, *that* was heaven.

We've been married seventeen years. Mark is still that smart, strategic go-to guy. He's no-nonsense on the outside, soft on the inside. I like to call him "the pillar of Jell-O." On paper, I never would have seen us as a match, but our differences are our strengths as a couple. It scares me to think how close I came to not going on that 9,001st blind date. I'm so glad I stopped being a control freak for thirty seconds and let my girlfriends convince me to reconsider!

GARTER BRIDE RAP SHEET: TISH RABE

Name: Patricia Annette Saumsiegle Rabe

Occupation: Bestselling children's book author, singer and television writer/producer

Married to: John Rabe

Kids: Two children with John; two stepchildren; one step-grandchild

Most nerve-racking dating moment: Telling John I *really, really* wanted to have kids . . . on our second date!

Words of wisdom for stepparenting: Always remember that you have something very important in common with your stepchildren: you all love the same person.

Greatest thing about being a Garter Bride: Looking up when my husband comes through the door and still not believing that he's really in my life.

I didn't go on 9,000 blind dates like Pat did, but there is a number that sticks in my mind: 52,560. That's somewhere near the number of hours I spent dating a man who had no intention of marrying me, even though he knew that I wanted to be married and have children.

He was much older than I was and had two kids. We spent hours over leisurely lunches, took weekend getaways—very New York, very romantic. I was crazy about him.

All my girlfriends who knew him told me he'd never marry me because he'd been married before and always said he'd never get married again, but that was like waving a red flag in front of a bull—it just made me more determined to make it happen. I'd show *them*!

Things started to get complicated when I could no longer ignore the fact that I really wanted to have a baby. Unfortunately, I was too young to be able to get up the courage to ask him how he felt about it at his age. If he'd said, "Yes, I want to have babies with you," I would have married him in a heartbeat.

The years went by and I was determined that somehow everything would work out. On the night of my thirtieth birthday we were sitting in a restaurant having dinner, and he told me he was very excited because he had finally found the right person to redesign his apartment.

And suddenly I got it. *Oh. You're redesigning your apartment—not our apartment. There is no "we" here. There never really has been.*

I got up and walked out. I'm only sorry I didn't throw my drink in his face because it would have been so dramatic. But in truth, it was my fault. When I started the relationship, I was young and got swept up in the romance of it all. Six years later, I was a grown-up—or should have been. Either I should have had the tough conversation with him or I should have had it with myself. But sometimes that's easier said than done.

I was so shaken up. I remember taking a cab home and thinking, *What have I done? Six years. And in all that time, our lives really didn't overlap.* It was one of those defining moments when you see the actual distance between yourself and someone you thought you were close to, and realize you're not really intimate. It was a hard fall.

Flashback: I met John Rabe when I was sixteen and he was seventeen. We were cast opposite each other as the leads in our high school production of *Oklahoma!*—I was Laurey and he was Curly and I thought he was fascinating.

On something like page 64 of the script (trust me, I'd flipped through!) he was supposed to kiss me. When you're sixteen and have braces, this is *huge*. But every time we almost got to that page, rehearsal would end! Finally one afternoon, I said my line, and he leaned down and kissed me. As far as I was concerned, that was *it*. The room sort of went quiet, as though everyone was thinking, *I dunno what just happened here, but it was something big.*

We sang in the same country rock band in high school, but after graduation we went our separate ways. After my big relationship breakup, I was living in New York and John was living near our hometown. He'd gotten married and had two kids, a girl and a boy.

We didn't meet again until years later when we both went to the same party hosted by a friend I'd run into at my high school reunion (which I almost didn't go to). He was separated and spending as much time with his kids as he could while also starting a new company. When I first spotted him, my old high school crush feelings bubbled up—it was almost as if no time had passed, though we both had been through so much. And there was no denying that he was having a similar reaction to seeing me again! He lived in Boston, so over the next year we flew back and forth just about every week. We used to say we should have bought stock in the Delta shuttle! But those long-distance trips made us realize how much we meant to each other and how our love was growing.

Because the kids were such an important part of his life, they became a big part of mine, too. I had lived alone for so long that it was a real adjustment for me to suddenly be part of a family of four. I remember going to McDonald's for the first time with him and the kids, watching him drive with one hand and eat a cheeseburger and fries with the other and wondering, *Am I ever going to be able to juggle a career and kids—let alone a cheeseburger—like he does?*

By this point, as you can imagine, my biological clock was ticking so loudly it was keeping me up at night. Somehow I managed to wait until the second date to blurt out to John how badly I wanted kids. I had learned the hard way not to make the same mistake in my thirties I had made in my twenties. I knew it was important to let him know how much I wanted to become a mom. Fortunately, he was willing to have more kids.

We got married in New York, and John's kids were the only ones in our wedding party, which was perfect. I'd had so many friends who'd taken years to get pregnant at my age that after we'd been married about six months, we began trying to have a baby.

We took a trip to visit his parents and I remember one morning joining everyone for breakfast in the kitchen. His mother was one of those eggs-bacon-and-the-works breakfast makers. I walked in and suddenly announced, "I would like some Baskin-Robbins Pralines 'n' Cream ice cream and a cup of tea." The whole kitchen hubbub stopped.

Our son was born on February 18, 1989. I was thirty-seven.

I was still writing thank-you notes for our son's baby gifts when I joyfully got pregnant with our daughter. She was born sixteen months after our son, just three weeks shy of my thirty-ninth birthday.

All four children are young adults now, and obviously we all made it through those early whirlwind years. That's one of the many lessons I've learned: things do change over time, and what seems impossible at first not only becomes possible but can be something that helps make you who you are in the best way.

I still have my *Oklahoma!* ticket stub (do I *ever* throw anything out?), and the night of our high school performance was February 18, 1969—the exact date of our son's birthday twenty years later.

When we were in high school, I used to hope John would say "Hi" to me in the hallway. To this day when he walks in the door, I can't believe that any of this actually happened. We are different in a lot of ways—I'm a night owl, he's a morning person; he's neat, I'm a clutter bug—but we both love kids, traveling, entertaining and spending time together. He's smart, generous of spirit and attention and takes care of his kids—and me—24/7. I am so lucky I was able to have the children I wanted so much and that we were able to combine our lives.

I still shiver when I think how close I came to having a lifetime of regret and letting time rob me of something that was so important to me. As I watch my daughter and my stepdaughter forging ahead into their lives (my daughter to college, my stepdaughter into marriage), I want to say to them, *Remember to ask yourself, "What do I really want?"* I learned the hard way not to wait for someone else to do that for me. I dreamed of having a happy home, children and a husband who loved me. And no one was more surprised—or thrilled—than I when those dreams came true.

GARTER BRIDE RAP SHEET: ANN JACOBS

Name: Ann Jacobs Blumenthal Jacobs (Jacobs was my maiden name, too!)

Occupation: Story editor and award-winning television producer with Pat Lampl, a partner in On the Aisle Productions

Married to: Irv Jacobs

Kids: Two stepchildren; five stepgrandchildren

Best wedding dress advice for grown-up brides: "It was my third marriage, but I refused to dress like a guest at my own wedding. I wanted to wear white, so I did."

Best quote from her husband: "Ann's a trophy wife . . . I got the prize!"

Most romantic thing Irv ever told her: "Every day's my birthday when I'm with you."

Greatest thing about being a Garter Bride: Never dreaming I could be so happy.

They say the third time's the charm, and that was certainly true for me in the love and marriage department. I'd been married twice: at eighteen (basically out of rebellion) and at twenty. My second marriage lasted for eleven years. After that, I focused on my career in film and TV production, which was creatively satisfying and involving, and I didn't really think I wanted to marry again.

You never imagine that your parent could fix you up with anyone you'd get serious about. But that's basically what happened to Irv. My friend Paula had taken a class with Irv's mom, Boz, and they rode the bus home together afterward. They became good friends, and I'd met Boz several times at Paula's home. One day Paula called me and said, "Boz's son just got divorced. He lives in Cleveland, but he comes to New York a lot, so I gave her your number." "What did you do that for?" I said. "What do I want with some middle-aged man from Cleveland? He's probably fat and smokes cigars."

No problem—he didn't call anyway. (Would *you* drop everything to call someone when your mother says, "My friend Paula has a nice friend, who . . ."?) My big selling point, apparently, had been that I was a good cook. Boy, did I sound like a winner.

Months went by. I'd just told a friend, "I want someone in my life, but I've dated every eligible man in New York and there isn't anybody. I'm just going to forget it and stick to my work and my friends, which are very rewarding."

Of course, the very next evening he called. (I later learned that every time he came to New York City, his mother would ask, "Did you call that woman?" Eventually he gave in!) I'd had a long day at work and all I wanted was to take a hot bath and curl up in bed with a book. But he said something on the phone that made me laugh—we laugh a lot—and I thought, *What the hell.* He was in New York and we met for dinner. He was tall and thin (and had never smoked cigars) and was one of those wonderful, naturally curious people. I loved his eyes—

they had a sparkle. We talked about literature, op-eds and Cole Porter. And best of all, there was instant chemistry!

I knew right away this man was going to be in my life. I think he did, too. Happily for me, he started coming to New York fairly frequently. When we first started dating, he told me that he was so excited at the prospect of seeing me that he didn't sleep the night before. After we'd known each other a couple of months, I had to go overseas on business. When I returned, he told me that he'd saved a message from me on his answering machine so he could hear my voice while I was away. I know very few men who would ever express those sentiments, even if they felt them. Since I'm rather shy, Irv's being able to share these kinds of things made me both trust him with my feelings and deeply treasure our relationship.

My work was centered in New York. Fortunately, he'd always wanted to be in New York, and his business could be pursued there, so he moved from Cleveland. Still, we kept separate apartments and didn't move in together. I think that mostly had to do with me. I'd been on my own a long time, and my financial and personal independence were hard-won and important to me. And with my marriage history, it didn't take Sigmund Freud to figure out that I was afraid of commitment.

Irv and I also have different personal styles, and that took some getting used to (you'll learn more about that in later chapters). He is much more extroverted than I am—"Just a few more minutes" is his usual plea at parties, while I'm longing to get home to my book. He loves tennis and skiing; I'm the original couch potato. I love to cook, and I yearn for a sous chef; he can push buttons on the microwave if given sufficiently clear instructions. I like to get things done; he likes to think things over—and we're that way about everything from buying a couch to balancing the checkbook to cleaning out our offices. What really makes us work is that in the end, our differences lead to a true meeting of mind and heart. Everything meaningful that we do together is enriched by our different perceptions. We enjoy the same things, and this is the first man in my life who loves to go to the ballet. He *gets* things; he *sees* things—the lighting, the costumes, the colors—that I don't see. He loves the news and I love history—the headlines of the past—and at breakfast we share what we've learned from our reading. He's interested in everything and up for any adventure. How could I not love someone like that?

Although we knew we'd be together permanently, as you'll learn later, between my independent streak and his deliberate decision making, it took us a while to get on the same page about getting married—ten years, to be exact!

Seventeen years later we still laugh at my brother-in-law's response when he heard we were getting married. He said to my sister, "I'll give the rehearsal dinner. After all, how often does Ann get married?"

Only when she knows that the third time's the charm.

To love and be loved is a gift a woman deserves at any age. It is this precious and beautiful gift that we seek for you.

A brief word to the wise: We're experts at being Garter Brides, but (as our husbands and children frequently remind us) we don't know everything. This book is not intended to replace the advice of qualified professionals. We all have times when we need some help—whether from a good financial planner, a lawyer, a therapist or someone else trained to assist and advise. Never think you have to handle things alone. A smart woman knows when to call in the troops. Let the pros deal with the tough stuff; let your girlfriends offer their true-life advice so you can live, love and have fun.

Now get ready to discover lots of grown-up relationship ideas, success strategies and inspiring stories that will make you smile, learn, hope and dream. Read on!

CHAPTER 1
Let's Take a New Look at Dating

Grown-up dating is different from dating in your twenties—in a good way! First, you're a lot wiser about what you want in a relationship. Second, there's only one rule: it should be fun. Both of you are looking for a new start, so give yourselves one! That includes your mind-set about dating itself. With the help of the Garter Brides, one woman reignited her dating optimism by calling a "blind date" a "first date." Now she goes out assuming she'll have a nice time and will want to see him again. Another woman stopped letting age keep her from dating: "No man ever thinks he's too old to date; why should I?" A third made a Declaration of Fun-dependence: she'd date anyone once as long as they were going to do something she'd enjoy. That way, she knew she'd have a good time no matter what.

An eligible mature man is looking for the same things you are: good times, companionship, great sex, sensitivity and intelligence— the kind of life you can offer! As the brides in this chapter confirm, those guys can turn up anywhere, and just because a guy doesn't fit your usual criteria doesn't necessarily mean he's wrong for you. One woman said: "I'm a buttoned-down type and Howard shaves his head and wears an earring." Despite their stylistic differences, she gave him a chance. Now they're happily married. As Ann notes, "It only takes one date to change your whole life."

So listen to your Garter Bride sisters as we tell it like it is. We hope our experiences will inspire you to continue seeking the love that's just right for you—because we're all proof that anything, absolutely anything, is possible.

Mastering the Mental Game

How can I keep from getting burned out on dating?

Boy, have we been there! Remember Pat resisting blind date number 9,001? Remember Ann telling her girlfriend she was giving up on dating—twenty-four hours before she met the love of her life? Remember Tish, who feared it might be too late to have a husband and family? We're thankful every day that we gave love one more chance.

What Do You Really Want?

You're looking for a man who really, *really* loves your uniqueness and who's truly worthy of how great you are. In short, you're looking for a guy who wants to brag about you. "Irv adores how smart Ann is," Tish says. "Hearts come out of John's eyes when he looks at Tish," Pat says. "Your husband talks about you all the time. He's crazy about you," a friend of Mark's told Pat. There are strong, secure men out there who want an equal like you. Here are some Garter Brides tips to find them:

- **Say good-bye to good-for-now relationships.** If your goal is to be married, you really must avoid relationships you know won't lead there. It's surprisingly easy to fall into comfortable but inconclusive dating: "The last guy I dated before meeting Kevin was a nice, casual relationship. He lived near me. There were no dramas.

I believe we lasted because it was too good to end and not good enough to get worked up about. We never had any conversations about 'us' because I think we both knew it was a good-for-now kind of relationship. Then Kevin came along, and I told this man I'd met someone I wanted to be exclusive with, and that was that."

This Garter Bride was lucky her good-for-now relationship didn't preoccupy her so much that she didn't recognize Mr. Right. Although these relationships can feel nice, they divert your energy from seeking a man you want to marry and who also wants to marry you. If you're in a relationship and think you'll stay until the right man comes along—it won't happen. You have to be emotionally available. "I was very discerning," one bride told us. "I knew what I wanted."

One bride shared an interesting perspective on why people engage in going-nowhere relationships: "I don't think people hold themselves back intentionally, but maybe from insecurity about going after something they really want. And I think this applies to men as well." You shouldn't make a decision about a relationship based on fear—fear of being alone if this doesn't work out, thinking there won't be anyone else. It isn't true. There will be somebody else.

- **Bad boys are time-wasters.** Not only should your man like bragging about you, but he should be someone you want to brag about. "When you want to get married, you don't waste your time on foolish men," says Gwen. "That means not getting involved with men who behave badly. Unfortunately, most younger women just don't get it until they go through that experience several times."

- **If you get advice, consider the source.** Your girlfriends may want to give you their opinions of the man you're dating, but if they say something negative, weigh their comments carefully. Some women have been so disappointed in their relationships with men

THEN VS. NOW

"In my twenties I was into the 'bad boy' thing. I was only attracted to men who were charming and sexy but distant emotionally. When I met my husband in my late forties I gravitated to other things—he was friendly, had a great smile and was a nice guy. I was looking for a companion interested in a long-term, committed relationship and was no longer willing to compromise what I wanted in order to have a man in my life. It had to be a more satisfying give-and-take relationship."

"When I was in my twenties, my mental checklist for guys consisted of 'attractive, tall, nice body, good dresser, likes to have fun.' I didn't really think much about the ability to be a good provider, what kind of a father he might make or his drive and ambition. Now those qualities are much more important to me—along with character, kindness, spirituality and a sense of humor."

"In my twenties it was about looks and chemistry. In my thirties it was about chemistry and substance."

"When you're twenty, you're growing together. When you're forty, you both know who you are. As established adults, you must be able to complement each other. It's important that your lives mesh. My husband is an active supporter of what I do."

"When I was younger I thought I had to downplay my career. I'd be working on big projects but wouldn't talk about them around men. By the time I met Mitch, I was comfortable just being me. If a guy liked me, fine; if not, not."

"When I was in my twenties many guys my age seemed more interested in dating unchallenging arm candy than in a woman with a brain. While dating again in my forties I was fascinated to meet men who were happy to forgo that kind of dependent relationship for one with a woman who can handle herself in all sorts of situations and who offers intelligent opinions and advice."

that they immediately focus on reasons for things *not* to work out. Only you know if there's chemistry.

■ *If your sex life has been on the back burner, heat it up!* Whether you're fresh out of a divorce or haven't dated in a while, make great sex a priority. Be open to enjoying a hot, healthy, abundant sex life with someone you love being with!

"If You Want to Get on the Train, You Have to Buy a Ticket"

Someone said this to Pat when she was feeling low about dating and finding Mr. Right. "It changed my attitude," she says. "I realized I could be tired of dating . . . but I still needed to date."

■ *Scanning dating websites is not dating,* the same way e-mailing your resume to a bunch of online job postings isn't really job hunting. Career coaches will tell you that networking your way into a job is much more effective. Yes, it's whom you know. More important, it's whom you *get to know.*

■ *Keep in shape for the big game.* "I always kept going on dates because it kept me out there and in practice," Judy said, "the way job interviews improve your interview skills."

■ *Spread the word.* "I told everyone I knew that I was dating and to please invite me anywhere there could be some guys to meet. I even said they should have their friends put the word out, too," Maureen told us. "A woman recalled a friend of mine saying, 'If you meet someone nice who's not quite right for you, remember Maureen!' That woman had just met a lovely guy, but she was already seeing someone. So she called my friend to ask if she could give this nice guy my number, and my friend called me. I said, 'Sure, why not? What's another date?' Ha! Little did I know! I married him!"

- **It's a numbers game.** The more dates you go on that don't work out, the more your odds improve of going on the date to end all dates! "I have friends who'd get so burned out on dating that they'd take a break for years! I'm good at setting goals, and my goal was sticking with dating."

- **Always go to parties.** It's the dating equivalent of showing up at the station to get the ticket to get on the train!

HOW THEY MET

"I went to a birthday party and noticed one woman who seemed very shy and was alone. I sought her out and spent the afternoon with her. About a month later, she called and said, 'You were so nice to me; would you like to meet someone I know?' I met him and I married him! So my motto is, always be nice to people. You never know how it's going to turn out."

"I went to a Labor Day party my mother was hosting. Her boyfriend's son was invited. It was love at first sight. It took another full year from that date before we had our first date, but the wait was worth it. I'd found my soul mate."

Meeting Your Match Online

How can I make Internet dating work better for me?

We've mentioned that finding the right person is a numbers game. As one woman said, "The Web is perfect for that. How many men can you meet in a bar? Online you can meet 3,500 in one night—anytime, at your convenience and it's anonymous until you're ready to change that. When you find someone you might like, you meet for coffee and spend twenty minutes with him, and if things don't click, all you're out . . . is the price of a cup of coffee."

"I think dating sites help you because making a list of what you're looking for in a partner clarifies things," another noted. "One of the things we had to share with each other was a list of five things we couldn't live without," a bride told us. "One of his items was 'love.' That really touched me." "Internet dating can be positive if you're shy," a Garter Bride observed. "I know a guy who says he'd find it hard to start talking to someone in a bar. Online dating helps you get to know someone a little before meeting them in person."

HOW THEY MET

"My sister took me aside during a family visit and confided that she and her husband thought I wasn't proactive enough about meeting men! I protested and listed how I'd tried to meet men. I also said I'd been on an online dating site. Well . . . that part wasn't true. That New Year's Eve, maybe partly because I felt a little guilty, I created a profile on a dating site. Jamie's was the first match that came up. He'd recently put his account on hold but had answered this one last time. It turned out he lived just a few miles away! We were married eighteen months later."

Whether you're into Internet dating or on the fence, we offer this advice from grown-up women who found Mr. Right on the information superhighway.

- "The good news is that everyone you meet in Internet dating is looking for someone—they want to find out about you just as much as you want to find out about them!"

- "Put in the time and stay with it consistently. Treat changing your life as a priority, with online dating as a means to that end."

- "The longer I did it, the more I could read between the lines for clues as to what the guys were like."

- "I generally just had men contact me. I was more comfortable with that; I liked feeling pursued."

- "Be thick-skinned. You'll put your profile out there and may not get as many responses as you'd like, or you'll respond to a profile and not hear back. As clichéd as it sounds, don't take it personally."

- "I looked for correct grammar and spelling in profiles and e-mails. I felt if someone's careless that way, they're not that serious."

- "I was completely honest on my profile. I think it's crazy to misrepresent yourself—who would want to begin with a disappointment?"

- "If you're feeling down about it, take a break—and then get back to it. Cheer yourself on, and get friends to cheer you on."

- "I didn't really follow the rules in creating my profile. I didn't go the 'I like walks on the beach' route. Instead I was very concise. In fact, a male friend helped me write it. For a photo I used a family shot with my parents! Harrison saw my profile and was intrigued. His initial e-mail to me said, 'It's clear that family is very important to you. I feel the same way.'"

- "Be specific about what you want. Personally, I wasn't interested in men who'd never been married. I felt they tended to have issues that went deeper than the ones divorced or widowed men have."

- "At first I didn't want to ask too many questions, but then I realized my shyness wasn't doing me any favors. I decided, 'I can ask; they don't have to answer.'"

- "For me, a photo of the guy was key—no photo, no date—although there can be exceptions (one was a doctor who didn't want patients to see his photo online)."

- "Some people don't want to post photos. In that case I'd ask them to send one. If they didn't, they were out!"

- "I didn't like his photo, but a girlfriend convinced me to pursue him. Thank goodness for girlfriends!"

- "Make your photo tastefully sexy—you at your most attractive, with a little lower neckline (not too much). I recommend a full-length shot. At first I posted what I thought was a nice photo. Then I posted one taken by a photographer—and got *many* more hits."

- "I put up a photo of myself that I loved because I looked happy in it, but I got no responses. A friend's husband saw it and said, 'That picture isn't doing you any favors! You're wearing a heavy coat and a big shawl. If I saw that I'd think you're the kind of person who tries to hide herself, and isn't open!' So we found a great head shot and as soon as I'd replaced the old photo I started getting responses. Amazing!"

- "Men may say, 'I hate to e-mail!' but I liked e-mailing back and forth at first to get basic information, the kind of stuff your friends would tell you before you go on a blind date—what they do, how long they were married, whether they have kids, etc. But after a week of that, if things were going well, then I wanted to set up a date; otherwise a false intimacy develops on e-mail and when you meet him you may be disappointed."

- "I found e-mailing back and forth frustrating—too much like pen pals—and wanted to cut to the chase and meet. I rushed the process and ended up having many more cups of coffee than were necessary!"

- "I noticed whether they were dependable. Do they answer e-mails in a timely way? Do they call when they say they will?"

- "For the meeting, I always met in a public place, preferably over a cup of coffee. That way we'd have some time to talk, but if it wasn't working, I knew it would be over soon."

■ "Be prepared to go on quite a few dates before you meet someone you want to see a second time."

40 MEN IN 40 DAYS: ONE WOMAN'S INVENTIVE APPROACH TO ONLINE DATING

If you're hesitant about online dating, the Garter Brides suggest that you make a plan of action with a girlfriend. One enterprising woman came up with a form of online "team dating" with a girlfriend and met forty men in forty days! Interested in volume business? Here's how it worked.

"I compiled a list of the qualities I was looking for in a man and suggested to my girlfriend that she meet half and I'd meet the other half.

"I met forty men in forty days. Meanwhile, my friend was meeting men, too. Sometimes one of us would meet someone who wasn't good for us, but we were sure would be good for the other.

"I went on to date fifteen men or so, some only once or twice. We really enjoyed it and did things like going dancing or going to sporting events. Then I met Andre. He was a widower who was just beginning to be ready to find someone again. We've been together three years."

Keep Your Checklists in Pencil

"The most common and superficial barrier to successful dating that I think men and women put up is the checklist," one bride told us. Some women find checklists very helpful. As we've said, it's a matter of finding the approach that's right for you. It is possible to be self-defeatingly picky, but if you really have absolute no-nos, stick to them. "Be true to your inner self," a bride advised. "If it's important that he be taller than you, admit it. You are who you are. That's the wonderful thing about dating when you're older: you *do* know who you are." Make your list of non-negotiables—but do it in pencil!

If he's the kind of guy you're looking for, he'll be keeping an open mind about you, too. "Mark had been married more than twenty years, lived in the suburbs in another part of the country and had built a certain kind of life there," Pat said. "He told me that one of the things that intrigued him about me was that I was very different from other women he had dated. He was open to getting outside his comfort zone, and we both allowed our relationship to develop."

Keep an Eye on Yourself

Now let's take a careful look at *you.*

- **How are you approaching dating?** Like a project? A task? A game? Choose a mind-set and a method that feel right to you, not because someone else says so. We know some women who approached finding a mate like a job hunt, and it worked for them. Sometimes a counterintuitive approach can balance out some dating habits that haven't been working well for you. "I tended to fall for the romantic rush," Bea said. "I needed to keep some distance and let guys pursue me more. That may not be right for every woman, but for someone like me, it worked."

- **Deep down, are you receptive or resistant to dating?** "For years I assumed I was no good with computers," Pat says. "I constantly worried stuff would go wrong. About a year ago I decided, 'This attitude is hurting me.' I signed up for a course at the local computer store. I realized I wasn't technologically challenged; I was technologically *resistant.* Once I took a different approach, I didn't fear technology anymore. I'm actually looking forward to the class on website design!"

If your attitude toward dating is a variant of "I don't like this/ I'm not good at this," guess what'll happen? Pat turned around her technophobic tendencies by saying, "I can be good at this." Once she became receptive, she began to enjoy it.

In an ideal world, our computers would always function perfectly . . . and Mr. Right would materialize as our seatmate on our next plane trip to visit Mom. Sometimes that happens! Even then, good fortune usually needs a push from us. As the saying goes, "Chance favors the prepared mind." So lift your head, open your eyes and venture out with finding him in mind. Then if and when Mr. Right *does* sit down next to you, you'll be receptive to striking up a fatefully fortunate conversation!

HOW THEY MET

"I'd just come from the gym, unshowered and sweaty—exactly the way you *don't* want to look when you meet your prince! I stopped at a restaurant, and the hostess asked if I minded sharing a table, because all the tables were taken. I said OK. That's how I met Brad!"

"We met as members of a bridal party: I was the maid of honor and Ian was the best man. He was married at the time, but I obviously made an impression because more than a year later, after he'd split from his wife, he called me! We started dating and I just knew it felt right."

- **Are there positive things you haven't been doing for yourself that you could be doing?** One woman needed healing time after a tough divorce. She took a break from dating, cared for herself through exercise, yoga and meditation, and worked hard to process the divorce. She returned to dating feeling "more developed as an individual, ready to relate to someone on a deeper level."

Another woman found her work helped give her confidence after ending a long relationship: "It gave me validation that I certainly wasn't getting from my ex. Having economic independence also helped enormously."

A third reflected, "I needed to become aware of how fast time passes and of focusing too much on my career, allowing my personal life to happen or not. I would never do that in my professional life."

How could you become the kind of person who dates effectively, calmly and positively? So many things have worked for the Garter Brides—read on.

Happiness Is Attractive

Emotions are contagious. The powerful, positive energy of happiness radiates to others and is highly attractive. "Do things that make you happy," one Garter Bride said. "Even if meeting a man is a priority for you, if you're doing other things that make you happy, it will shine out from you. I go ballroom dancing. I never met anyone doing it, but I love it! If I didn't have a date on a Saturday night, I didn't sit at home; I went dancing. I was happy because I was doing something I love."

"Reece and I had worked together at a very small company. Even after we left for other jobs, we kept in touch and got together now and then. One year I threw myself a birthday party and invited Reece, whom I hadn't seen in a while. I was having a ball at my party and loving the world that night. My happy state must have triggered something new in Reece, because he invited me to his place for dinner the following week. I asked him, 'Is this a date? A fling? Or just friends getting together?' 'A date,' he said. We had a wonderful evening and were married two years later."

HOW THEY MET

"I met my husband when I signed up for flying lessons—he was my instructor. I flew with him once a week for a year before we went on a date. I always liked him and even developed a little crush at one point. Still, I was surprised when he asked me out—and shocked at the sparks when we hugged good-bye after our first date. Within a month it was evident the relationship was serious. Three months after our first date we started a premarital counseling program at the church I attend. We got engaged when the class ended, four months later."

Leading a contented life as a single woman is good for marriage, too: "I've learned that a key to a happy marriage is not only to find a wonderful man who lifts you up instead of squashing you down, but being able to enjoy your own life."

Check Your Anger at the Door

I have a history of dating disappointments, and sometimes I'm really critical of men. How can I drop the bitterness and give a new guy a chance?

As Garter Brides, we know women who are bitter about ever finding a mate, or about being divorced or wronged by men. We know you don't want to go there. "Being optimistic is key," Carrie believes. "If you're feeling discouraged, take a break—stay off the Internet dating sites for a while. Take the time and be good to yourself, perhaps by reading some helpful books or talking with someone professionally. I feel you have to like men in order to date productively, not be furious at them. No matter how attractive, pulled-together or accomplished you are, if you're angry it's not going to happen."

THANK GOODNESS FOR GIRLFRIENDS!

Our girlfriends were (and still are) godsends. When we were dating, we kept each other sane, laughed and cried together and encouraged each other. "My girlfriends were always there for me as a support system and to do things with," Molly said. "We compared notes about our lives and I valued their judgment. I loved that they were doing interesting things. We also made sure our time together didn't revolve around going out looking for guys or talking about dating all the time."

If you have a girlfriend who's really down on men, despite your bringing it lovingly to her attention, try steering the negative conversation in new directions (she may get the point), focus on doing activities together (i.e., less complaining time) or if necessary limit your contact. Carrie continues, "I actually avoid women who are constantly bitter and angry with men because it does nobody any good. Even if they're justified in how they feel, they'll be better off if they get beyond it and make a happier life for themselves."

Anger can damage lives. A Garter Bride says, "My friend Sally was very angry after her divorce (her ex-husband got remarried six months later) and vowed never to get married again. She was pretty, smart and funny, the sort of woman who should have been surrounded by kids, grandkids and a man who loved her. But her inability to get past the old hurt derailed her chances for love."

We've been inspired by hearing Garter Brides describe how even the most broken hearts can open to love. "I had traveled home with my two daughters to visit my parents right after I'd, once again, found my then-husband with another woman," Marie told us. "To say the least, I was devastated and exhausted. The next day we bumped into Hank, a casual friend of my parents', and we chatted for a while. A couple of months later my kids and I returned for the Fourth of July and the family went to a big barbecue. My seven-year-old daughter, Jeannie, recognized Hank in the crowd and brought him over to our table. My parents ended up taking the girls home after dinner and Hank and I stayed out until four in the morning! We both knew that this was something special. The fact that my shy Jeannie spotted Hank and asked him to have dinner with us was just amazing. Hank had taken an interest in Jeannie the first time we'd met, and that had made a big impression on her. I guess you could say that Jeannie was responsible for bringing us together."

"You Never Know"

If your mom said this to you about meeting guys, she was right! Pat laughs: "At intermissions, don't go to the ladies' room. Even if there's only a million-to-one chance of meeting Mr. Right, I guarantee it will not happen in the ladies' room—and if the line's long, you might not even get in! So go beforehand. And at intermission, have a drink at the bar . . . because *you never know!*"

For the same reason, Tish says, "Go to high school or college reunions! Going to mine was the last thing I imagined myself doing, but a few of my girlfriends were going, so I figured, 'Why not?' I hadn't been back home in years, and it turned out to be fun—plus, reconnecting with my high school friends led to my running into John again. Other Garter Brides have met their husbands the same way. It could happen to you!"

HOW THEY MET

"My mom and I were on the shuttle bus going to the beach. Randy had the seat in front of us and asked if he could tip it back. We fell into conversation. I thought he was very cute. When we got to the beach we exchanged cards. I asked my mom, 'Do you think he'll call?' He called the next day, and we met for a drink. I knew right away he was special."

"One morning I was meeting a girlfriend to go shopping. I got to the store early, so I went inside to buy something. I was waiting in line and a man got in line behind me. We started talking, and he asked if we could exchange phone numbers. It was instant chemistry!"

"I'd been through two painful breakups and felt I'd never meet anyone. I was focusing on my acting career and performing in a show. Someone I worked with had friends come to town to see the performance. I met with one of them, Quinn, to give him information about local hiking. Later we played pool at a bar in town. We had a good time, he seemed nice and I started to like him. That night a group of us went out after the show. So there I was in sweats with soggy hair—and Quinn and I felt comfortable together. He asked if he could take me (and my poodle) to breakfast the next day before he left town. I did, and guess what? My dog threw up all over his car. But he was so good about it. I just knew it was right and so did he. We dated long distance, and after a year he proposed."

"My fun, eccentric friend, Sandi, and I were going to a movie and she needed to stop at her apartment first. Her new roommate, Edwin, was there. I was immediately attracted to him—he was so handsome and had a twinkle in his eye. After chatting awhile, he and I went by ourselves to the movies and then talked till three in the morning in a local watering hole that had the worst but cheapest wine in town! Now we're married."

Here are some ways to put "you never know" to work for you:

- **Hang with your married friends.** A happily married couple is most likely to fix you up with guys because they want others to be as happy as they are. Between the two of them, they know more available (or soon-to-be-available) men. "Married lovebirds are inspiring!" Ann says. "A friend of mine had been divorced for several years. She dated, but always had a pessimistic attitude about men and long-term commitment. When Irv and I decided to get married and she saw how happy I was, I believe she rethought her own feelings. Within a year she was engaged and very, very happy." Another bride noticed, "After I got married a number of my single friends got married—two at forty-seven and one at forty-three. I like to think I was their inspiration!"

- **What about work connections?** Workplace romances can be complicated, but as one bride says, "Work friends can be good matchmakers if they know you well." Few of the brides we interviewed found their husbands sitting at the next desk, but if you go to office parties, the spouses of your coworkers can be a source for fix-ups!

Sometimes romance on the job blossoms when you least expect it: "I traveled to do a film project and Joel was the studio technician. After spending six hours together in the editing room, we started to make small talk and hit it off. When I asked him about things to do in town, he offered to take me on a guided tour, which included a spaghetti dinner and a nighttime view of the city from the tallest building in town. Who would have thought that a studio job would have led to my happy marriage?"

Romance can also happen between people who used to work together. Remember the bride who threw herself a birthday party and fell in love with her former coworker Reece? "I think we knew we were right for each other so quickly because we'd worked together so closely in that small business. We'd seen each other feeling happy, stressed, successful and rotten with a head cold. And we already knew how to operate as a team."

THEN VS. NOW

"When I was younger, my marriage criteria had more to do with finding a man who fit society's or my parents' idea of a good catch: good provider, father potential, handsome, athletic. Now what counts is being able to communicate with him."

"I met my husband when I was thirty-seven and he clearly wasn't what I'd been attracted to previously. Historically I gravitated to powerful guys or soulful arty types. My husband is a very lovely, sensitive, non-aggressive, approachable guy."

"I think it's wonderful to date a man who's been married before. His first wife helped him get used to living with a woman. My husband is a very sharing person."

"At twenty I envisioned a house in the suburbs, two perfect children, no financial problems, no fights, no difficult in-laws. I never gave one thought as to how any of this was achieved or if this was what I really wanted, versus what I thought I was *supposed* to want. When I married later, I knew I wanted a man who was confident and wasn't still 'finding himself.' I wanted someone who appreciated the things I enjoy, who had a sense of humor, who respected my feelings and ideas, and with whom I would have a good and happy sex life!"

"When I was twenty-two, my list was simply that someone be handsome and interested in me. Once I hit forty I wanted a partner—someone to share life's ups and downs who can make me laugh, who gets me."

■ *Similar backgrounds can be a plus.* Tish and John grew up in the same hometown, and such common history can be the basis for a comforting familiarity. "Vince and I met online, but it turns out we were both raised in the same faith and both our families have roots in the West. I think there's something to be said for having similar backgrounds."

- *The perfect partner may not look perfect on paper.* As we've said, just because he doesn't match all your criteria doesn't mean he's wrong for you. Heed the Garter Brides: "If you'd put our relationship on paper, you'd have said it would never work. Mark wanted to be in a satisfying relationship, but did he want to remarry when we met? *No!* I was at a point where I wanted to get married. What a loss if I'd decided not to go out with him because I assumed that he wouldn't want what I wanted." Another noted, "Just because someone's newly divorced or separated doesn't mean they're emotionally unavailable." Said a third: "Would I have chosen someone who was fourteen years older than me? No, but I was open to it."

Dating Outside the Box

Now let's talk about the date itself. Our Garter Brides gave us lots of ideas and stories of how they dated smart and found Mr. Right.

First-Date Jitters Don't Happen on the Second Date!

First dates can be stressful as we try to manage first impressions: *Do I like him? Does he like me? Did I just sound stupid just now? Am I talking too much? Does he like his parents? Is he nice to the waiter?* And on and on!

Guess what? He's doing the same thing! "I met Al online. I liked his picture and he sounded thoughtful in his answers to questions. But our first date did *not* go well. He just kept talking and talking. He didn't ask me anything about myself. I actually said at one point, 'Do you have any questions for me?' He said, 'Well, I don't want to put you on the spot and make you feel uncomfortable,' and I said, 'Oh, no, you need to ask them.' Finally at the end of the date, as I was about to get in my car, I was looking at him hoping he'd ask for another date, but he just kind of stared at me and said 'Good-bye.' And off I went.

Ten minutes later he called me and said, 'I had a really good time. Would you like to go out again?'"

Given that you're both a little nervous, if you suspect there might be chemistry, think of the first date just as a pathway to the second one: *Whew, that's over! Now let's get to know each other!*

DIVIDE AND CONQUER!

If you go out with your girlfriends to meet men, the best way to stick together is to stay apart. Divide that room and conquer it! Fan out and circulate. Men are more likely to approach you if you're alone. Keep in touch with your girlfriends during the evening and text them if you're leaving. Later you'll all have fun comparing notes and stories.

"Hmm . . . Tell Me More!"

On that first date, consider yourself a social explorer. One bride always reminded herself, "I may learn something about myself, people or the world." Don't think marriage. Just relax, hang out and have a good time. As one bride said, "At the very least you'll have a great story!"

"When I met Ray, I was actually seeing a few men, though none seriously," Debra said. "I had a date in the afternoon before meeting Ray for a drink. I was running late and called the restaurant to say I was on my way. When I got there he was relaxed and nicely dressed, and he rose to meet me—low-key, grown-up and a gentleman. Our drink turned into dinner. He asked what my favorite movie was and I said *Gone with the Wind*, because it was the story of a self-centered girl who became an interesting woman. I could tell he enjoyed this exchange, which made me relax even more. I talked more and revealed more than I normally ever would on a first meeting—and that was good. I was more authentic. Normally I'd be more aloof."

Here's other first-date wisdom from our brides:

- *Try to have no preconceptions or expectations.* "When my future husband called to ask me out, I didn't have anything to do that night, so I agreed. I went with no expectations, and that's when good things can happen. We knew right away we really liked each other."

- *Look your best.* When you go out, looking great will make you feel better and boost your confidence.

- *Keep it about the two of you.* Don't bring up aging parents, bemoan your teenager's angst or bash your ex. Get to know each other first.

Tired of the Same Old Date? Do Something!

It's said that kids open up more to their parents during a side-by-side activity like driving in the car, taking a walk or working together on a hobby. It's true for grown-ups, too! It could be bowling, miniature golf, strolling a street fair, going to the circus, taking a tango lesson, enjoying an amusement park, going fishing, volunteering at a walkathon, hiking a nature trail or attending a sports event. A shared activity gives you something to talk about, laugh about and have in common. You'll also pick up interesting info about him as you work or play together: How collaborative, competitive, creative, insightful, easygoing, kind, resourceful or funny is he?

HOW THEY MET

"I was *not* going to meet this guy for a tense dinner at a restaurant . . . so we went to a hockey game! He brought his mother and his brother; I brought my sister and my mother. Afterward, we all went out for burgers."

"A couple I know asked me to dinner with their widowed friend. We arranged a date. The next day, Dominick called. He said he really wanted to get to know me before our dinner. He suggested a drive in the country that weekend. I agreed, and he said he'd pick me up at nine in the morning. I said, 'No, too early,' so we decided on ten. (It was our first negotiation: he's a morning person, I'm not!) On a first date you really get to know someone much more than you realize. We stopped at a diner for a sandwich and I could tell he enjoyed food but wasn't fussy about it. I also learned he was a man who knew what he wanted and went after it. He told me later that the moment he saw me, he had an instant feeling that this was right and thought, *I'm going to spend the rest of my life with that woman.*"

"I was visiting a company in California about developing products for teenagers and I kept hearing, 'We can't agree to anything without talking to our boss, Simon.' The team sounded intimidated by him, so I pushed for a face-to-face with him myself. When I met Simon, all I saw was a smart, thoughtful guy—not scary at all! We were both going to San Diego after the meeting, so he gave me a ride. We talked nonstop about books. By the end of the drive, I'd asked him to dinner—though he claims *he* asked *me*!"

Everyone says, "Do things you're interested in" to meet guys. I've taken classes and joined clubs. I've made new friends but haven't met the man of my dreams. Any advice?

You should absolutely do things you like to do—but we agree with the bride who said, "Don't sign up or do things only to meet guys. I found that never worked very well, though I met a lot of cool women to do things with and through whom I could meet men. But it doesn't work on any level unless you're doing something you have a passion for."

Speaking of passion, Ann says, "If you love food and cooking, take an evening cooking class—not the how-to-boil-water variety, but the real international stuff. I found it full of newly divorced men who wanted to learn how to manage in the kitchen."

The local Y and adult education courses offer all sorts of interesting and affordable experiences—scuba diving, dancing, golf and yoga, to name a few.

Not Your Mother's Blind Dates

In your twenties, getting fixed up was uncool: your mother would set you up with guys she approved of and you never liked them. No wonder blind dates get a bad rap. But two of the three of us met the love of our lives on blind dates—so we're here to say that grown-up blind dates should be seen in a new light.

Blind Dates = First Dates

As we've said, think of a blind date like a first date: simply a get-to-know-you to see if you want to see him again. As Ann says, "It's one evening of your life. If you don't click, you never need to see him again. On the other hand, it may be the last date you'll ever need to have. Remember, he wants to meet someone, too. You're both hoping something wonderful will happen."

Preapproved by Your Friends: What's Not to Like?

Sometimes our friends know what's better for us than we do. If a friend thinks you should meet a particular guy, consider him pre-screened! "When I felt ready to date after my husband passed away, I said to a friend, 'How will I meet someone new in a town of only 4,000 people?' Chad and I were fixed up by friends. It was a first blind date for both of us. He hadn't dated at all since his divorce a year or so earlier. We both knew right away that we were right for each other."

Any blind date can have a happy ending. "Sal and I were introduced by a mutual friend who hosted a barbecue to create an opportunity for our meeting. He'd been told he was meeting someone 'with a French name'—so he spent the whole time talking to a woman about my age named Jeannette! Jeannette's husband suddenly appeared on the scene, and Sal and our hostess disappeared for a clarifying conversation. He left right after that, and his warm and friendly good-bye to me took more words than he'd spoken to me the entire afternoon. Our hostess later explained the name mix-up. Although I was annoyed (was he *that* out of it?), I was already intrigued. Two days later, he called to invite me out for dinner. We ordered the same thing. We talked. I was smitten. Three more dates and we were in love."

Try a Second Date

We love this idea so much that we propose you make it your new rule for dating! Here's the story of how it happened.

"My friend Cecilia's boss wanted to fix up his best friend, Jake, who he described as a terrific guy who'd been tragically and suddenly widowed four years earlier. He asked Cecilia if she knew anyone who might be a match. She thought of me.

"Since Jake was a quiet type, they made me promise I'd see him more than once. I agreed because I didn't want Cecilia's boss to be mad at her! "We went out and he was nice, but I felt he was too mature for me (he's eight years older) and very quiet. I didn't feel any sparks, but Cecilia insisted I go on a second date. On the second date he was far more relaxed and had a wonderful sense of humor. Best advice I ever took! And we've lived happily ever after."

This story also proves our previous points: your friends know you like no other, guys don't always ace the first date either and the first date is *only* about deciding if you like the guy enough to see him again. By the second date you'll both be relaxed enough to give each other a truer picture of who you are.

Made It Through the First Few Dates?

Enjoy it! And consider these ideas, which our Garter Brides used to build and deepen their relationships:

- **In the age of speedy everything, feel free to go slow.** If your relationship is solid, it'll stand the test of time, distance and busy schedules. Said one woman, "Our schedules were crazy and it took us more than two months to meet in person after we met online. We phoned each other and e-mailed a lot. By the time we got together it was very comfortable since we already felt connected. We'd bypassed the getting-to-know-you conversations and really hit it off." And another: "I just wanted to be friends first, which we were for about three months, doing a lot of group activities together. In the process, we met each other's friends and everyone seemed to get along well."

■ **Know what to overlook.** Pop quiz: Which of these would you choose to overlook? "A girlfriend told me she didn't like her date's fuzzy eyebrows!" "I dated a guy who would turn on the stove burners to heat his apartment because he didn't have to pay for gas— and he was making a good salary!" There's much in between these two extremes, of course. Use your well-developed common sense and decide what's really important to you. Said one bride: "I really, really love him. Sure, he has faults—but so do I."

■ **Recognize a keeper.** Here's where your grown-up people smarts pay off. When you see the fundamental qualities you seek in a life partner, you'll know it. This bride did: "Appreciate him and let him know it. If he's come out of a bad marriage, his ego is shattered." Another commented, "The weekend after our second date, he offered to drive us to the beach for the day. He drove two hours to pick me up, two hours to the beach, two hours to get me back home and two to get to his home. He spent eight hours driving just to spend an afternoon with me. I was stunned that he'd go so out of his way. I wasn't used to someone being so considerate. I remember thinking, 'This is a nice guy, and I deserve it.'" Here's another: "He did everything right in our dating relationship. He didn't go too fast or too slow. He called dependably. He had garden-variety baggage like everybody does, but no huge issues. It sounds kind of old-fashioned, but he was proper. I knew he was special."

Love is a gift at any time, but there's a special sweetness to falling in love later in life when, as one bride said, "You know better who you are and what you need to be happy, and are freer to give yourself in the right way." You appreciate a man who's willing and able to give of himself in partnership: "He's even-tempered, generous and loved by everyone. He makes my life easier in many ways. He was well worth waiting for!"

You relish the privilege of having a true partner: "He's the first one I want to talk to about things." And you're aware of how special every-day life becomes when shared with another: "I think my favorite part of being with him is when we come home to each other, saying, 'Hi, how was your day?' It's just very romantic. We love seeing each other, we love eating together and watching our favorite TV shows or movies together. It's just so cozy and domestic." Another bride said, "When I'm driving in a storm I like someone to care that I get home safely. I like caring about someone and having someone care about me."

We know that the special man who cares especially for you is out there, as he was for us. Our fellow Garter Brides know it, too: "Never give up on believing you'll meet someone and become his wife. I never knew I could love someone like him or be loved by someone like him." All of us believed in and looked for lasting love—and found it. You can, too.

CHAPTER 2
We Really Like Each Other! What Now?
Taking Your Romance to the Next Level

It's official—you're a couple. Others are starting to see you that way, but most important, so are you. The more you're together, the more in sync you feel. It's thrilling and even a little dizzying. You've waited a long time for this fabulous sensation—enjoy it!

Maybe you've been seeing each other for a while, or maybe you knew right away that this man was going to be important to you. Either way, your feelings are starting to deepen and there are things about your lives the two of you need to talk about if you think you're going to have a future together.

Maybe you each live in places you love many miles apart, or have demanding jobs and all the responsibilities that go with them. Maybe there are issues with exes or with wounds from past relationships. Maybe one or both of you have children. Maybe you want children and your biological clock is ticking—when do you have "the talk" about that? Each of you has a history; now you're preparing to build one together.

When a grown-up man and woman begin to put their heads and hearts together, it's time for you to talk about the past, share your present and confide in each other your hopes and dreams for the future.

THE FOOD OF LOVE

We asked our brides: "What was the first thing you cooked for him, or he cooked for you?" Their answers proved there's no accounting for taste when in love!

- "Grilled cheese and salsa on English muffins—which burned because we were kissing!"

- "Soft-shell crabs."

- "He prepared shrimp in radicchio cups. (Guess who does the cooking in our house!)"

- "The only thing my husband ever made me was lime Jell-O."

- "Veal cutlet, and I made him think I'd slaved all day over a hot stove."

- "Mozzarella and tomato on a baguette."

- "I took him to his first Indian restaurant. He'd never had Indian food, but after his first bite he looked up at me and said, 'My taste buds are dancing.' He's been an adventurous eater ever since!"

- "He roasted a filet of beef *en croûte,* and that's the last thing he ever cooked for me. I keep asking him when he's going to do something else!"

- "The first thing he cooked for me was chicken—which wasn't terrific, and my son said, 'Gee, it tastes just like the chicken Henry makes.' Henry was my previous boyfriend!"

Is He "the One"?

You're well past the getting-to-know-you stage, and it keeps feeling more and more *right.* You may notice signs you're starting to think exclusive. "I realized I'd stopped checking my online dating website and had cancelled a date with someone else," one bride told us, "because I'd lost interest in meeting other men." You feel you can call him just to say hello, without a pretext like "I have tickets to a concert. . . ."

Your thinking is getting more future-oriented. You see a travel ad and imagine vacationing together. You feel you could ask him to a family event. Perhaps most telling, you've both started saying "we": "I didn't know you liked bluegrass music. Next time that band's playing, we'll go." "My brother's a baseball fan, too. Maybe we could all see a game." "It's too hot to go hiking now, but we could go in the fall when the trees are turning."

Sometimes the feeling that he might be the one grows almost imperceptibly until suddenly you realize it's there. In the Introduction Pat talked about her "aha" moment in the park, when she realized she wanted to talk to Mark about her work problem, he called as promised and she felt so supported by their discussion: "That's when I knew I'd turned a corner with Mark—and in my own mind about what was important in a relationship. I'd always thought that love was drama and anxiety, and I finally realized that it should be my safe harbor."

At other times, those who love you are the first to see the signs. Claudia and Peter each had been married twice, and Claudia was hesitant about falling in love again. "After we'd been dating a few months, my parents and sister were visiting, and I invited Peter to join us at my place. He loves to cook and brought food he'd prepared.

"When I overheard him telling my mother, 'She's so smart and well-read,' it hit me that he had real feelings for me, although he hadn't said so yet. Shortly after that my mother came into the kitchen and said, 'You need to realize this man is really serious about you.' At this point I was still ambivalent about being serious with anyone, but it helped me to see that he'd made up *his* mind, even though he hadn't yet expressed it directly to me.

"Since we both had such busy weeks, we always scheduled a Friday night date. One week, though, he had to have some minor surgery. I took care of him and enjoyed it. It made us feel closer." Bit by bit, as they did the caring things couples do, their relationship was growing.

How do I know he's the one for me?

Here are some of the ways our brides knew:

- **Can you be yourself with him?** "By the time I met Ron, I was comfortable just being me," said Ellie. "Like me, he talks a mile a minute, and every day we do about twenty different things! With him I can be who I am, which is so liberating. In your thirties you're more comfortable in your skin, and even more so in your forties."

  Marsha said, "In the first six months I dated Drew, I shared things I never discussed with my former husband, who was competitive with me and tried to keep me in check. Drew was a partner."

- **Do you like how he listens ... and talks?** Does he understand what's important to you—your values and interests? Does he share what's important to him? "I want a man who has empathy," Annette told us. "Someone who not only listens when I share personal things but contributes and shares his feelings. If I'm worried about one of my kids, I want to be able to express that and have him really respond and contribute ideas. When I was younger, someone who would just listen was OK. Now I'm with a man who listens *and* has insight. What a difference!"

  Pamela recalls, "Once I was telling a guy I was dating about a work problem I was dealing with, and he said sarcastically, 'Boy, that's some way to earn a living!' Needless to say, I never saw him again. I'm so glad I found a man who doesn't diminish what I do and who appreciates my accomplishments. It's essential if the relationship is going to work."

- *How does he handle relationship problems?* "We'd both been hurt in past relationships and needed to learn to trust again," Liane said. "We rode through all the bumps of that process with each other. Now I can't imagine not having had that to bind us."

  "We talked about living together and he wanted me to move in immediately, but I said I wasn't ready yet, and he respected that," Benita recalled. "That added to what I liked about him. It took me a while to feel ready, and he didn't push, he just hung in there. He got a lot of points for that in my book."

- *Is he a man of his word?* Does he deliver on what he promises? Does he call when he says he's going to? "With Julian, there was no game playing," Jane told us. "Just a really nice person who, when he said something, meant it."

- *What kind of man is he?* How does he handle stress? Is he fundamentally good to others? How does he treat his mother, other family members, friends and servicepeople? "Paying attention to the little things a man does will tell you a lot about him," Dina advised. "My ex was horrible to restaurant servers. I should've seen that as a sign of who he was." "When I saw the way Will acted around his young nieces and nephews, I thought he'd make an excellent father," Sondra said. "He's kept in touch with his inner boy."

- *Is he there for you?* When Katie met Cam, she'd been divorced for fifteen years, enjoyed her freedom as a medical technology sales rep and liked having her space. One day after they'd been dating awhile, she was in her car when a truck backed into it. She wasn't hurt, but she was shaken and returned home. "I called Cam to let him know what happened. He left work and came over to be with me. That's when I knew he was someone special and that I wanted him in my life permanently."

Siobhan "just wanted to be friends" with Dan—which they were for about three months, doing a lot of group activities together. In that time they met each other's friends and everyone got along well. "Then one day there was a series of burglaries in my neighborhood that was all over the news. Dan called me right away to make sure I was OK. Somehow that did the trick. I realized what a wonderful person he was and that he exhibited qualities I found important—loyalty being a top priority."

Of course, being there for someone is a two-way street. Men need help, too, and it's a mark of true maturity when they can admit and accept it. "John's parents were in their seventies when we met, and they were having more and more health problems," Tish says. "It was stressful, and I was glad to listen and help however I could. It made me feel great to be able to lighten his load."

Our romance got very hot, very fast. The sex is great, but I want to make sure we're right for each other outside the bedroom, too. How do I pull back a bit without blowing it?

First, regarding the hot sex: enjoy it! The Garter Brides are unanimous about this: good sex is essential in a relationship—raw, fun, sweaty, steamy, quickie, crazy, funny sex . . . tender, knowing, comforting, slow, drowsy sex . . . rainy-morning, summer-evening, first-day-of-vacation, happy-anniversary, kids-are-at-camp, because-we-still-can (and want to!) sex. And let's not forget makeup sex! This is the time to revel in the attraction you feel for each other.

As you start doing more things together, you'll learn whether the relationship is going to work in the long haul. Just be sure you *are* doing things outside the bedroom, exploring common interests and other kinds of fun to share! It's OK to enjoy all the excitement as long as you're checking in with your grown-up common sense to make sure you aren't losing your head along with your heart. You've worked hard to get where you are in life, and making big, hasty changes can have serious consequences.

We and other Garter Brides found that the pace of our relationship naturally slowed as we started combining our complex lives. For example, if either of you has children, your dates and overnights might be scheduled to coincide with when the kids are with their other parent. Child rearing is a clear priority that everyone needs to put ahead of date night. Scheduling this time also gives you a chance to talk honestly about your custody arrangements—including how you think the kids might react to the idea of having their parent involved with someone new.

GARTER BRIDE TIP

NOBODY'S BODY IS THE BODY IT USED TO BE

If you feel the least bit critical about your body, news flash—nobody's body is exactly as it was in their twenties, and that includes the wonderful man in your life. Yes, some of us found younger men, but for those of us who love men our age or older, they, too, aren't quite the Adonises they were years ago. But that doesn't mean we all aren't still hot and very, very desirable. As one Garter Bride's husband said, "Men are pretty simple. If we like you, we want to sleep with you—it's just the way we are." So celebrate that wonderful truth and enjoy the passion you feel for each other!

"When I met Ethan, he was driving six hours every weekend to visit his daughter," Shari recalls. "I'd found the love of my life, but I was still home alone every weekend! But one reason I loved Ethan was that he took his family responsibilities seriously. So when he was away I made plans with friends, ran errands and visited my family. The pacing changed again as his daughter started visiting us sometimes, and eventually went off to college. Planning our time together was the first example of how good a team we could be."

You both probably have other activities, too (work, classes, working out, volunteering, home chores, errands and so on), plus friends you want to stay in touch with. As you get to know each other, you'll settle into a rhythm that works for both of you. Neither of you should stop doing the things you like in order to be together; be yourself. If you're not into watching *Monday Night Football* but that's how he unwinds, set up your yoga class for that night or get together with a girlfriend. Keep being the active, interesting person he's falling in love with. Remember you'll have lots of time to develop mutual interests.

If you feel the need to slow down because you're ambivalent about the relationship, by all means take a step back. While many Garter Brides told us both they and their partners knew quickly they were going to be significant in each other's lives, many others weren't sure at first. Some feared being hurt (again); some loved the freedom of being single; some were falling for a different type of man than ever before and needed to get used to how that felt.

"There was a disparity for a while in our feelings for each other," Amalie said. "I wasn't ready to commit to Brandon. There were certain differences between us. For example, it wasn't like we could talk for hours on end. He could be a little socially awkward at times. He wasn't quite the ideal I'd pictured. So I put on the brakes for a while. But eventually I realized I was so comfortable with him. Every weekend we'd stay in and watch movies. We'd talk about the week, and it was just wonderful and relaxed. He was so nice, so sweet. In time I couldn't imagine life without him. It was like I turned a corner and decided,

'This is what I want. This is for me. I like my life with this man. It feels good and it feels right.'"

Getting in Your Own Way?

What do we know about self-sabotage in relationships? Some of our brides spent years dating men who were disinterested in marriage, yet hoping they'd propose. Pat waited for Mr. Unavailable to become available. She observes, "When you start to have serious feelings for someone, there can be a lot of fear along the lines of 'I hope this relationship doesn't disappoint me' or 'I hope I don't screw it up.' One of my self-sabotage patterns was to pursue men who weren't emotionally available. If I dated a nice guy, I'd start testing him or pushing him away. Guess who wasn't being emotionally available? It was as though I was undermining the relationship to avoid being disappointed."

Take a good look inside and see if there are any self-defeating patterns in your love relationships. Here are some insights from our Garter Brides:

- "I had to allow myself to be happy and not screw it up."
- "When you're older, you've had time to complete yourself as a person, so you can see what kind of person you need and want to be with."
- "Being a mature bride (and groom) has its advantages. Both Eli and I knew what we needed and wanted as individuals. We don't look to each other to fill some emotional gap. We are able to look to each other for companionship and fun."
- "I still have the same personality that I did in my twenties, but I have more insight into my behavior. I know all the indicators that might sabotage myself."
- "I let myself be adored, and I let myself enjoy it. That was a big thing for me."

Now may be a great time to look at your other relationships through this positive lens. Happiness has a way of spilling over and enriching everything in your life. As you nurture this precious new love, it's a perfect opportunity to make new beginnings and ensure your other relationships are running as they should. As part of that, you may find that some people who are more acquaintances than friends naturally fall away, partly because you have less time now than you used to. But as Pat says, "Lifelong friends will remain just that! My friends will always be an important part of my life, and they know it."

Meeting the Children, Part 1

If one or both of you has kids, now's the time to get a conversation started about how you might bring them into the picture. We call this section "Meeting the Children, Part 1" because the first part of this process is just talking it over. There are almost as many ways to handle this as there are kids—in fact, much depends on the individual child.

For now, you want to simply tell each other about your children with tenderness and honesty. What are they like? If they've had to deal with divorce, how have they handled it? What's your gut telling you about their reaction to your dating? Do they know about this new person in your life, and if not, when do you feel is the right time to tell them?

As you do this, you'll find out where your feelings and opinions intersect or diverge. If the kids are still living at home, one of you might feel OK with the idea of spending the night with the kids there; the other might not feel the kids are ready for that. The point is not to determine whose approach is "right"—these issues are complex and very personal. The point is just to share your feelings about the when, where and what of the process. It's also an opportunity to learn about each other's instincts and priorities when it comes to parenting. That way, you don't have situations where, for example, he says, "Hey,

I rented a cabin at the shore for the long weekend; we could all go," and you have to say, "No, it's too soon for my kids." Or maybe you're the one picturing him and your kids exploring the beach and getting to know each other, but he's not ready to become involved like that yet. With some honest conversation, you might realize that an afternoon at the circus is a better idea for everyone.

"There's Something I Need to Tell You . . ."

You're having a great time together, but you may also be wondering when to bring up certain serious complications in your life. It might be a health issue, a family problem or something else you feel is very private. You don't want to make a big deal of it, but it's something a significant other should know. Worrying about how much to say, when to say it and what to say? Here are some general considerations we've found useful as Garter Brides.

Determine When and Whether It's a Need-to-Know

There are certain things in our lives that only our nearest and dearest need to know. Deciding when you feel it's time to share this information with the man in your life requires some careful thought. In these days of television reality show confessions, very little is considered shocking. But shocking and private are very different issues. If it's personal to you, that's all that counts.

Details of your past relationships need not be part of your present conversations if they're not pertinent to a healthy relationship between you. "There were certain areas of our lives Irv and I didn't discuss," Ann says. "For example, we didn't delve too deeply into our previous marriages. Going over what went wrong didn't contribute to what we were building together. My main concern was that I get along with his children—that was very important in our current lives."

You're both adults and it's expected that you had a life before you met each other, so there's no need to lay your soul bare. He fell in love with the person you are, and your history is what made you who you are today.

Even something that does affect your partner, such as a personal health issue, can be shared in a way that puts you in charge of the situation. "I've had bouts of depression since I was a teenager," Isabelle told us. "I told Justin when we were pretty sure we'd be in each other's lives forever. I've encountered people who have no understanding of depression and confuse normal ups and downs with clinical depression, which is devastating to the person experiencing it. I can wake up one morning and feel like life is over. Nothing sets it off; it just happens.

"Telling Justin wasn't easy, but I knew he needed to understand that there might be times in our lives when this would occur. I also made sure he knew I was working with an excellent doctor and managed it well.

"At first Justin couldn't comprehend how I could be so down as to be unable to function—especially since he knew me as an incredibly competent, positive person. It took a long time for him to finally understand, but it meant everything to me that he always *wanted* to understand. I've had two bad episodes since we've been together. He tries to help, but what helps me the most is knowing that he's quietly there and will support whatever I feel needs to be done."

If you and he are having future-oriented conversations, think about what's going on in your lives that could affect the two of you. As Isabelle said, "I didn't want him to think I was keeping something from him, or that I sprang it on him." Whether it's about debt, health, work or an ongoing family situation, the question is not whether he'll help, or even perfectly understand, but whether he'll be sympathetic and supportive as you navigate the situation.

Be Careful of Oversharing . . .

"Women may think they're bonding by confiding, as they do with other women," Ann says, "but that's not necessarily how it works with men."

Many women have been fed the fantasy that men will "take care of them." And we've seen some pretty smart women buy into this. Wanting the relationship to be "for keeps," a woman will share personal matters, hoping that it will deepen the man's involvement in her life and help cement the relationship. Unfortunately, this also can lead to confessing private matters that, if the relationship ended, you'd seriously regret revealing.

We certainly don't advise that you keep secrets, but do take time to ask yourself some questions about what you're planning to disclose:

- Is it something that he should know if he's going to be around permanently, but not something that will have a day-to-day effect on our time together?

- Is it something that, if it comes up, can't be taken care of without disrupting our life together?

- Is he discreet? Can I trust this man with my confidences?

- Will he offer advice, and if he does, how will I respond to that?

- Is our relationship on a solid footing? If we end our relationship, will I regret his knowing this information?

- Am I making too much of this?

. . . but Don't Wait Too Long

"It's pretty obvious you should only tell someone very private things if you trust him completely," Ann says. "But there's a point where you *must* tell him because if he's going to be in your life and you wait too long, he'll wonder if the delay means you didn't trust him." What's the middle line between too much and not enough?

If you're facing ongoing stress with your ex-husband, it's a good idea to give your partner a heads-up: "Listen, if I'm a little distracted, it's because I have to take my ex back to court." And the conversation can go from there.

If you have an addiction problem, it is certainly a serious issue, which we hope you're addressing. If he has one, the same applies to him. But any prospective partner has a right to know in order to consider the impact it might have on his or her life. That's why full disclosure is a must. The same applies to sharing financial challenges (debt, job loss, lack of health insurance and so on).

Hard as these conversations can be, these days there are few things people find truly shocking. The problem may feel bigger to you than it does to him. Remember his life, too, has had its ups and downs. In a mature relationship there's history on both sides. Most of us have become more accepting and mellowed with the years.

Just remember he's not your therapist, girlfriend or lawyer, and don't let "stuff" start to overtake the adventure and wonder of your relationship. "Most of us have a lot of responsibilities," Ann notes. "And guys have their share of stress, too. We can offer each other insight and support from our years of life experience, and we should. But our relationship should also be a place of refuge and fun."

A Baby . . . Maybe?

My biological clock is ticking! When and how do we have the "Do you want to have kids" conversation?

By the time Tish met John, her biological clock was in alarm mode! "Somehow I managed to wait until our *second* date to ask him if he'd be willing to have more kids. At the time, his children were four and six. He said he'd like to have two more, but he wanted to do it fast because he didn't want to run after a two-year-old when he was fifty. I was a TV producer, so schedules were my business. I pulled out a calendar and did the math!" They weren't married long before they were overjoyed to welcome a baby boy and a girl into their lives.

Although Tish's second-date strategy may not work for everyone, we do believe the desire to have children runs deep in those who want to become parents. If that's the case for you or him, this conversation should be a priority once a relationship becomes serious.

"I broached the baby topic when Mark and I had reached the point where we were exclusive—that is, both of us were having future-oriented conversations along the lines of where we might live," Pat recalls. "We weren't engaged and he hadn't proposed, but if he had, I'd have said yes. I was in my late thirties; he was in his early forties and had children. I remember saying that I thought we were really good together and that our relationship felt great to me, *and* that although I didn't mean it should happen this very second.... Basically, I fumbled my way into saying that if he couldn't entertain the idea of having another child, then continuing our relationship was a bad idea for me.

"He seemed a little surprised by that. (And I thought I'd been so clear about my wishes by saying how much I *loved* children!) He gulped and said he'd think about it. I said, 'I understand why you might not want to be a parent again, but this means a lot to me. I'd like to keep talking about it.' If I'd overreacted at that point and abruptly ended the relationship, we'd never have made it to where we are now—happily married and the ecstatic parents of our daughter."

So, what are we saying here? We're saying that we believe it's necessary to strike a balance between having the baby conversation early because you know it may be a deal-breaker issue and deciding that if you don't get exactly the response you want in the first conversation, there's no future for your relationship.

On the first side of that equation, as Pat found out, indirectness doesn't cut it. Don't imagine that expressing your deep love of children communicates how important becoming a mother is to you. And even if he's a doting uncle or father, that doesn't necessarily mean he wants to be a parent (again). As one Garter Bride said, "Don't assume because someone loves kids they want to raise them."

If you absolutely want children—whether biological or adopted—this is one grown-up issue where time is *not* on your side. "There are very few ships that sail in life," Tish says. "If you don't like your job, your home or even your mate, you can quit, move or get divorced. But once the baby boat is out of the harbor, it's gone. If you wait too long, you may be too old to have a child or make an adoption plan. I have girlfriends who waffled on this decision until it was too late."

It needn't be a heavy conversation initially. In the course of doing things together, there's no reason why you can't say that at some point you want to have children. That gives him time to think things over and doesn't put him on the spot for an immediate answer.

Later, find a relaxed time when you have his full attention and find out how he really feels about becoming a father. (Yes, it'd be great if the guy would bring this up, but don't count on it, because he likes you a lot, too, and may not want to broach a possible deal breaker any more than you do.)

If he already has kids, he may feel he can't imagine starting over with a newborn, or he may fondly remember raising his kids and want to have more. If he doesn't want to have kids and you do and you think, "After we're married, I'll change his mind" (we have friends who thought this, too), we urge you to ask yourself with unflinching honesty: Will not having children be a lifetime regret for either one of you, and if so, how would that regret affect your relationship?

NO KIDS, AND OK WITH IT

Not everyone wants children, and that's a perfectly acceptable place for a couple to be, if they're both there together. "Kevin and I met when I was thirty-eight and he was forty-two, and it was a first marriage for both of us," Erin said. "Neither of us wanted to have children, and we've never regretted our decision. We feel privileged to devote our lives to each other. Without the financial strain of having kids, we have the freedom to take on work and community projects that are important to us."

"I was forty-eight when I met Gabe, and when we married, he said it would be OK with him if I wanted to adopt a child," Gina said. "I teach grade school and I love children, but I didn't feel having children was the right thing for us. We have lots of kids in our lives, and that's enough for me."

Where Are We Headed?

Is your goal marriage or bust? Or would you like to live together first for a while? One bride we know laid her questions and wishes right on the line: "I asked him if he had any sexually transmitted diseases, and both of us got tested. I asked him why he'd gotten divorced and also told him I didn't want to keep moving (he'd been in the military and had moved a lot during his first marriage)—that I wanted to find a place where we could live, and stay there."

These are very personal questions, and as with the issue of having children, women vary widely on how they feel about these topics. We urge you to find the time that's right for both of you so you can happily deepen your bond with your man, free of worry.

"My boyfriend asked about living together, and I said no," Tina said. "I'd done the living-together thing in my twenties and learned I was capable of sharing my life with someone. In my thirties, I didn't need to do that again. I told him, 'The next guy I live with, I'm going to be married to.' And we were!"

"When I met Edward, I knew immediately he was someone special, but I'd been divorced for twenty years, had raised two children and liked my independent, single life," Greta told us. "I would've been happy spending weekends and a couple of days during the week with him. But he wanted to be with me almost all the time and kept talking of our future: 'When we do this, when we do that . . .'

"One night in a restaurant, he was talking about 'when we're married.' I said, 'You never asked me.' He said, 'Would you like me to?' When we left the restaurant, I thought, *Oh my God, am I engaged?*"

We told you there was a broad spectrum of opinion here! So, figure out where you are, where you want to be and how important it is to you that he be right there with you.

I adore my guy, but he's been through a lot. I feel like I'm half therapist, half sex goddess. I'm loving the sex-goddess thing, but how should I handle the half-therapist part? And are there any red-flag issues I should be aware of?

To answer your first question, it's not that you don't want your guy to confide in you about what's going on in his life, but you shouldn't confuse intimacy with responsibility. You can be supportive and helpful without taking the problem on. You need to take the time to figure out a role that's appropriate and comfortable for you. It's also possible that he simply needs to vent about what's going on in his life. It's cathartic for him, not necessarily intimate. It's one thing, for example, to listen to his frustration because court dates were again changed for his child custody hearings, but you both need to set limits on how much time you spend on those conversations. One bride we know told her boyfriend one morning, "I don't like having breakfast with your ex-wife."

While couples in their twenties mature together as they face different life situations for the first time, couples meeting as grown-ups are already mature—or should be—and have a big toolbox of life skills and a large network of resources to draw on, from friends to books to professional advisers. "If you tend to take things on more than you should, that's work you have to do on yourself," says Pat. "If he's doing the traditional male thing of delegating the emotional caretaking to you, that's work *he* has to do. As a new couple, you have to learn to share your ideas, to understand what's important to each other. That's what's going to make you a good team."

Red flags may range from debt or spending problems to substance abuse or emotional troubles that impair your relationship. If there are problems, you're probably starting to notice them. Whether they're deal breakers for you is a personal decision. Advising on these issues is beyond the scope of this book, but as a starting point, consider these questions: How does he handle problems in his life, and in your relationship? Does he ignore, withhold information, deny or get angry when you try to discuss any concerns? If he says he's going to deal with a problem, does he?

The good news about being a grown-up is that you're aware of problems that may crop up. Pay attention to your antennae and make mature decisions.

Making Time for Having Fun

I thought the hard part was meeting Mr. Right, but it's turning into Mr. Not Right Now. We're both crazy busy— demanding jobs, family obligations, friends, volunteer work and on and on. How can we make time for each other along with all the other things we have to do?

While you're not living together (yet), now that you're a couple you'll both need to make some modifications in how you've been doing things. Scheduling your love life is just the way it has to be when you're not a teenager anymore. We schedule time to hang with our girlfriends and do other fun things and don't think, *It shouldn't be this way.* We think, *Wow, I'm really looking forward to seeing Sue on Friday!* Ditto when you make plans to be with your man. You'll feel aglow all week, anticipating that happy time you're going to spend together!

If one or both of you is divorced and has children, your overnights will likely be organized around visitation schedules or the time when kids are with the other parent.

If your schedules are truly hectic, you may need to talk about limiting or curtailing some activities in order to give your love the nourishment it needs. "When Mark and I were dating exclusively, he had visitation two weekends a month and served in the Army Reserves one weekend a month, leaving us very little in-person time," Pat says. "He was eligible for retirement from the Reserves and when we discussed it he decided to take that option. As much as he loved being in the Reserves, our time together was more important."

Absence Makes the Heart Grow Fonder?

After vowing I'd never be in a long-distance relationship, here I am. The logistics are nuts, but I've waited so long for the right man; I don't want to break things off. How can we make it work when I'm here and he's there?

All three of us were in long-distance relationships with our true loves, and many of the brides we interviewed fell in love with men who lived anywhere from several cities to a continent away. (In fact, we know brides who've forged ecstatically happy long-distance *marriages!*) We won't kid you that it's easy, but you know that already. You'll need to be very clear with yourself on how much this man means to you, because even your friends and family may worry: "My closest girlfriend and my mother weren't sure at first it was going to work out for Fritz and me. They couldn't see how anyone could have a relationship with all that commuting." Here are our tactics for bridging the miles with smiles:

- *Make it mutual.* "If Mark was going to a city near me on business at the end of the week, I'd sometimes drive or take a train to meet him, on my own nickel. That way he wasn't always the one coming to see me."

- *Make it fun.* Turn a liability—the long commutes—into an opportunity: use your frequent-traveler miles to plan a little escape together.

- *Meet in between.* If you can afford it, meet up someplace between your respective locations.

- *Budget with care, and put technology to work for you.* Long-distance relationships can be expensive, so agree together on how you're going to budget things. Nowadays, technology helps couples bridge the miles: texting, videocam and voice over Internet protocol (VoIP), or whatever the geeks invent next, can let you stay in touch with ease and speed in ways couples couldn't do even a few years ago.

- *Plan nesting time.* Sometimes your time together is so intensely romantic that it seems like an extended dream date, where you're on your best behavior and trying to make great memories to sustain you during times apart. "While a couple who's local may need a getaway retreat to unwind and romance each other, a long-distance couple may need to bring things down to earth in a nesting kind of way," Pat says. For your vacations, maybe you rent a cabin and cook together, gather firewood, take hikes and make each other breakfast. Or you do a volunteer project together, working the finish line at a charity walk or serving meals at a shelter over a holiday. Or take a "staycation" where you spend time in the other person's home. Get the mail, walk the dog, load the dishwasher. Live inside the other's life for a week. When you do, you'll feel much more in touch with each other's lives from a distance. Also, it's a nice break from the expense and stress of travel.

- *Enjoy the spaces in between.* As one bride said, "In the weeks I'm alone I spend time with my girlfriends, eat popcorn and an apple for dinner and do all the things I used to do when I was single." If you're a parent, these periods often give you opportunities for quality time with your kids.

Ain't Love Grand?

We end this chapter with memorable romantic moments that we and our fellow Garter Brides have experienced with our husbands. With new love warming and growing in your heart, we know there'll be many such moments in store for you!

- "When something good happens in my work life and I share the news with my husband, he always says, 'I'm not at all surprised.' When we say good-bye before leaving for work and I'm facing a hard day and say, 'Wish me luck,' he says, 'You don't need luck.'"

- "When I'm feeling down or overwhelmed by something and find myself getting tearful, my husband hugs me and says, 'You're my girl.' And I am, and it calms me right down, because I know we're in this together."

- "Years ago we took a memorable summer road trip through New Mexico, driving through vividly colorful landscape, and at dusk we'd eat fabulous southwestern food in tiny local restaurants and share an ice-cold beer. Now when we go out to a restaurant and one of us says, 'Want to share a beer?' it's always with a little special glance that says we both remember that wonderful trip and how much fun we had—and still have—together."

- Mark and Pat exchange romantic cards "not just on the anniversary of the day we met, but every month on that day. It's a nice pause in the middle of our hectic lives."

- "I'll never forget dancing alone on a terrace after our wedding."

- Whenever John picks Tish up from the train station, she tells us, "even if I'm only carrying a shopping bag, he gets out of the car and comes up onto the platform so he can carry it for me."

- "After our wedding, we walked hand in hand up Fifth Avenue on a beautiful April evening."

- "On Valentine's Day we get in bed with a chocolate soufflé and two spoons!"

- Tish says, "For our fifteenth anniversary John and I renewed our vows so the kids could be there and share the event with us. We met with the minister ahead of time and she asked us, 'What do you love about each other?' I told her that John is the most giving person I've ever met—he takes care of me, the kids, the house, the car, his job, and spends all his time making sure things go as smoothly as possible for all of us. When she asked him what he loved about me, he said, 'I love everything about her.'"

- "One week I had to travel and while I was gone there was a huge snowstorm at home. I was dreading getting off the train to dig out my car, which I'd parked in the lot. When I got there, I found every car covered in snow—except mine! It was dug out and brushed off. When I opened the passenger door, I found a note on the seat that simply said, 'I love you.'"

■ "I've always been a big believer that it's the little things that show someone that you love them. My mother once told me, 'Folding laundry shows people you love them.' When I was younger, I had no idea what she meant, but I get it now. When I fold laundry and put it away for everyone, I know that when they open the drawers and see it they'll know it's a sign of love."

■ "One thing I think is important to remember about love at an older age is that nobody's perfect. You're not, he's not, who is? You know how to accept each other and work around whatever it is that might not be perfectly aligned. I'll be the first to admit, I'm not a gourmet cook. Somehow I've managed to get meals on the table for my family, but it's an ongoing challenge for me. A few months ago I was telling someone that I don't consider myself a fabulous cook and John immediately said, 'But she makes great soup!' And you know, he's right!"

■ "I just walked into the kitchen, where Irv was eating lunch. He looked up and said, 'You're so beautiful.' Not bad, after twenty-five years together!"

CHAPTER 3
Who *Are* All These People?
Friends, Family, Exes and Everyone Else

Maybe you've been dishing about your man to your friends and hinting to your family that you've met someone special. Or maybe you've kept this treasured relationship a bit private. Either way, you've got a wonderful feeling this guy might be right for you.

When two people get serious, friends and families are part of the package—and for some of us, that can be a pretty large package! So let's talk about going public with your guy.

The Garter Brides' Guide for Going Public

How can we make sure things go well when meeting each other's friends and family?

Although this relationship really only needs to feel right to *you*, of course you hope the people you love will love each other. As Garter Brides, here are some guidelines we used when we and our mates started to mingle:

#1. You Know What You're Doing

At this point in your life, you've successfully navigated all kinds of relationships. As Pat says, "If I feel myself fretting over a relationship that's not going the way I hoped, I remind myself of what I know: a combination of caring strategy and time usually wins."

#2. Remember Everything Is Connected— and There's More of It!

When your life changes, so do the lives of the people around you. This big change in your life naturally affects them, so if they need some time to get acclimated, don't worry. Also, there are simply more people to consider, as the fabric of grown-up life is richly textured: "Between the amazing friendships I've made with coworkers over the years and the great people I've met through my community work, my social network is broad and varied," one bride said. You want your partner to participate as much as possible with the people in your life. That process, too, takes time. So let it!

#3. "Anything I Need to Know?"

Are there things about your loved ones that you should alert each other to, to help everyone get off on the right foot? For example, is Mom a lovable yet incurable control freak? Do you and your brother "get into it" sometimes? Clue each other in so you and your man are working as a team.

#4. Think of It Like a Date

We know, we know; you thought that was over—and it is! Now apply some of your winning dating strategies here, including checking heavy expectations at the door. For these first meetings you want a positive first impression, a nice time together, with interest in getting to know each other better. Two other great dating tactics: keep the first meeting relatively short, and hold it at a neutral place. More first-meeting ideas follow.

#5. Call a Girlfriend!

Sometimes people don't hit it off. That's life. You're in control of how you respond. One Garter Bride shared this quick way of keeping her cool: "Ross's mother is very critical, and though Ross and I knew better than to buy into it, staying calm wasn't easy! Sometimes I called my girlfriends beforehand, or even from the ladies' room if things were really rough. They'd always commiserate and get me laughing, and often they gave me good ideas for getting through. It also really helped me to imagine recapping with them and telling them how I'd handled things—hopefully well! Connecting with my girlfriends gave me instant perspective."

#6. Confide with Care

"I had brunch one Sunday with some women friends, and naturally we got into the subject of the guys we were dating," Robin told us. "Two were old and trusted girlfriends; the third was a recent friend and business colleague. Geoff and I had been going out a little while, but we certainly weren't etched in stone. One night we ran into my new friend at a movie (she didn't have a date, which I'm sure made it difficult for her). When I introduced her to Geoff, she practically screamed, 'Oh, I know all about you!' I could have strangled her. Geoff looked puzzled (I didn't clarify), I was embarrassed and I realized that it was way too early in my relationship with Geoff to be talking to anyone but longtime trusted friends."

Samantha's boyfriend was working out a complex alimony agreement, and it was an emotional time for him. Samantha occasionally let off steam by confiding in her girlfriends. "Jason knew

I was talking to my women friends, but he had no idea it was, like, primal scream therapy!"

It's OK to lean on your girlfriends. We do it all the time; that's what friends are for! Just make sure you can trust them to be super-discreet. Before they meet your boyfriend, gently remind them of what you shared in confidence. Everyone will thank you for preventing questions like "Have you got a court date yet?"

#7. Pencil Things In

Your friends and family plus his friends and family equals . . . a full calendar! It's a happy problem when you have to consider someone else's schedule while making plans. Before finalizing plans with others, take a few minutes to coordinate with your mate. If you tell someone, "That date works for me, but let me see if Dave's free" and later say you can't make it, Dave may be viewed as the wet blanket. "Thanks for thinking of us! Let me check our calendars and call you tomorrow" is the better way to go.

"When I was first dating Mark and he lived in Atlanta and traveled constantly for business, my calendar was definitely etched in pencil because it changed so often," Pat recalls. "But I was thrilled to juggle spending time with a great guy alongside my hectic career and social obligations. It felt so great to be entering a room not by myself but as a couple. I loved having 'scheduling calls' with Mark, because it was about finding ways to be together and enjoy each other."

Meeting Friends

Our friends are our extended family. As one bride says, "I visit my parents twice a year; I have breakfast with my best friend every two weeks." We can't imagine what our lives would be like without our amazing, accomplished, wise, wonderful and wacky girlfriends. We've shared dorm rooms, demonic bosses, double dates, dark secrets, holiday dinners, countless parties, mornings-after and probably seasonal flu. Our friends are our grown-up family, which is why our peer group is often the first to meet our new love.

We're ready to meet each other's friends. What's the best way to make sure everyone hits it off?

Many of our Garter Brides shared stories of dear friends who introduced them to their new love, were the first to see love blossoming and aided and abetted the process right up to and including joyously witnessing the wedding day!

Of course you want your friends to see all the terrific things in your new love that you do. But (thank goodness!) you're no longer at the age where "it's all about the boy." You're not about to choose between the two. "I wanted to keep my full life going," one bride told us, "and my friends are a huge part of that." Here's our advice for getting the good times started:

- **Trust everyone's good intentions.** Your friends want what's best for you—otherwise they wouldn't be your friends! "My friends knew how much I wanted a husband and children," Tish says. "When I started introducing John around, they were thrilled, but some weren't sure how I'd do as an instant stepmom." "My friends wanted to like Irv and Irv wanted to like them," Ann says. "Everyone put their best foot forward."

- **Decide together whom to meet first.** Introducing your best friend to your man first might be the best way to go—or it might feel like a blind date in which *three* people have to hit it off! Some people feel more comfortable one-on-one than in groups, so talk to your boyfriend and determine what's best for your situation.

■ *If you start with a group, decide on larger versus smaller.* Social gatherings become more intimate as they get smaller. A lively open house isn't as intimate as a Sunday brunch, which isn't as intimate as dinner with another couple. At larger gatherings you can arrive and leave spontaneously and interact more casually, compared to more structured sit-downs that can have an "interview" feeling. So work your way from larger to smaller. Go together to a friend's Saturday night party. Then meet a smaller group for drinks. Then have dinner with a close (or best) friend, who's probably already met your mate at one of these larger gatherings.

■ *Find a focal point.* Find something interesting for all of you to do. Meet your best friend or a few close friends for a movie and talk about it later over pizza, go to a baseball game, go bowling, take a walking tour, share a picnic at an outdoor concert, go apple picking, volunteer at a community event. You'll all get into the spirit of things and have something to talk about.

What if some of my friends don't like him?

Your opinion is the only one that counts. But our girlfriends have seen us through thick and thin (including the pounds), so it's natural to want everyone to get along. "I've had some friends since I was six," Katrina told us. "Now I was thirty-eight and introducing them to JJ, and I really wanted them all to get along."

If your girlfriends don't whisper to you, "He's great!" after the first couple of meetings, ask yourself the following questions:

■ *Is this a new type of guy for you?* Pat recalls, "Mark was such a different type than I'd ever gone for. He was fun and good company, but he wasn't an unavailable bad boy. He was a grown-up, a secure man who loved that I was smart and independent. Although he's a softie inside, as a military guy he has a commanding presence and is very direct. There was an adjustment period for my friends to get used to my making a better choice about the kind of man who was right for me."

■ **Is envy in the mix?** Some of your single girlfriends may be truly happy for you, but seeing you in love reminds them how much they want this for themselves. Give them time to adjust and make an extra effort to connect and do things one-on-one. Ultimately, your having found a great guy at this stage of your life should give your girlfriends hope that they can, too. "When Mark and I had been married for several years, we had dinner with a girlfriend and her boyfriend," Pat says. "It was a wonderful evening filled not with small talk, but with what I call 'big talk.' They were both divorced— he had a young son and she a grown daughter, and, of course, they had their exes. They were very concerned about making this complicated setup work. They married a year later (she wore the garter!). At their wedding they told us that they decided to get married after our dinner together, inspired by our approach to our life and our love for each other. Needless to say, Mark and I were humbled and thrilled. But I don't think we're alone in helping grown-ups couple up: another friend told me that after she got married, three of her single friends over forty did, too!"

Men may be competitive. Alexa told us, "When Jared and I had dinner with a close girlfriend of mine and her husband, the husband was so rude to Jared that he said afterward, 'I will never see him again.' When I was younger I was always trying to smooth things over. Now I said, 'You're right.' My girlfriend and I do things when our spouses have other plans. I think she knows why, though we never talked about it. Unfortunately, I suspect this isn't the first time it's happened."

Ann recalls: "Irv and I went to brunch and a matinee with a recently married friend whose husband I'd only met once briefly.

At the intermission, they made a point of not getting together with us. We obviously hadn't made the cut with him. She and I still meet for a girls' lunch a couple of times a year, but no foursomes. It's fine with all of us!"

■ **Is fear in the mix?** A girlfriend may worry that your new love will take you away from her. Tell and show her how much you value her and all the great times you've had together. Make a point of planning get-togethers that don't include your boyfriend—for breakfast, coffee, yoga class, a manicure or other activities you both enjoy. She'll realize that even if you're a bit preoccupied as you transition into your relationship with your boyfriend, her friendship still means the world to you.

■ **Is there a grain of truth?** Maybe he's nervous and trying too hard, or has a manner that can be off-putting until people know him better. "Sid is 135 percent a salesman," Vicki told us. "When you first meet him, he comes off as a sales guy. Some people thought he was really shallow until they got to know him."

Even if your girlfriends are in some respects right about their impressions, that doesn't necessarily make him wrong for you. Also remember they just may not see him as you see him . . . *yet*. Keep in mind that all of them are going to be in your life for a long time and they'll have plenty of opportunities to get to know one another.

Even if they don't click, as Garter Brides, we've found that grown-ups find ways to work things out. That's what Tara, Marcus and Lori did, despite Tara making just about every mistake we warn against: "When Marcus and I were getting serious, I was so excited I wanted to introduce him to family and friends all at once. It was probably too much of a whirlwind, but fortunately everything went great—until Marcus met my best friend, Lori.

"Lori and I had been friends since high school and practically spoke in code. But it was clear in the first fifteen minutes that the man I loved and the friend I loved were not going to love each other.

"In the months I'd been dating Marcus I'd told Lori a lot about him, but what I *didn't* do was tell Marcus enough about Lori and the crazy-wonderful friendship we'd had for almost twenty years. I think the most I said was, 'You've *got* to meet my best friend.'

"When we met for dinner (just the three of us, which I later realized put them both on the spot) I saw that Lori is an extrovert with a zany sense of humor, whereas Marcus is more quiet and reserved. I had naïvely assumed it would be love at first sight. It wasn't.

"Lori and I still see each other and go out without Marcus; our friendship is as close as ever."

THANKS FOR (NOT) SHARING

Well-meant advice may come from family and friends, but you understand your situation best. Usually we make a neutral reply, like "Thanks. I'll give that some thought," or the quietly honest "Thanks, but I feel good about this."

"One of my longtime guy friends said we were rushing," one bride told us. "He wondered if I really knew my husband and said jokingly, 'Does he really know you?' He told me I needed to slow down. I told him that I'd been taking flying lessons with my now-husband for a year—trusting him with my life in a plane I didn't know how to fly—so I definitely felt I could trust him! You can learn a lot about a person quickly when you're in the cockpit together—like how they deal with adversity, what they expect of themselves and how they handle stressful situations. Not only did I see those things in my husband, but he'd seen them in me—so he knew some of the worst of me, in my opinion."

Some of our friends are single, some are married and we're all busy. How do we make time for everyone?

The sisterhood of our girlfriends is precious to us and always will be. We've all been married awhile now, and with the perspective of years we find our friendships can withstand periods where one of us temporarily drops out of sight in the whirl of daily life. When we *do* talk or meet, it's amazing how bonded we feel after just a few minutes of laughing, confiding and catching up. E-mail helps us connect between visits. "No matter what happens, always keep up with your girlfriends," a Garter Bride wisely said. "Yes, my list of friends has narrowed now that I'm in a committed relationship—I can't keep up with everyone and I don't travel with my girlfriends anymore. But when we get together, it's great."

We're sensitive to our single girlfriends' feelings about our being attached and do things our married girlfriends did for us when we were single. We often meet them to see chick flicks or attend a museum exhibit of special interest to us. Sometimes we meet for breakfast before work, or for dinner if our husbands are working late or out of town.

A number of grown-up brides we know advocate some separate socializing on principle: "If you want to go out with work friends, your boyfriend might be bored to death with all the shop talk. Also, you can encourage him to go out with his friends."

GARTER BRIDE TIP   ABSENCE MAKES THE HEART . . .

Doing some things apart means you'll have adventures to share when you come back together. It keeps you spicy and interesting to each other. And as one bride says, "Keeping part of your lives independent makes it even more special when you spend time together."

Many Garter Brides found that their friendships with married couples deepened with shared couple experiences. "It's been such fun to go on double dates and travel with other couples," Pat says.

Some of his friends talk nonstop about old times and people I don't know. I feel excluded. What to do?

We bet if you ask your boyfriend, he'll say you sometimes slip into this mode with your girlfriends! While reminiscing is a great way to appreciate each other's history, there's a limit to what's appropriate. We all have a past, but we're engaged with making new memories now and want friends who are on the same page.

"Irv had a lot of old friends in Cleveland, where he used to live," Ann says. "I'm delighted when we get together and they update him on who's doing what. However, a couple of people treated me like I was 'temporary' and Irv's real life was not with me. So after the initial updates are over, I make a point of bringing up something he and I have done together recently. If we all have a shared interest, I ask about that, or even what recent movies they've seen. Fortunately, Irv wants to move on, too. A quick catch-up is fine, but he'd just as soon talk about things relevant to our current life. At twenty I'd have found this focus on his former life upsetting—I'd have felt rejected and taken it way too personally. Now, at most I find it mildly annoying and take steps to change it or just ignore it."

Some friendships that were wonderful in the past don't really fit our present, as Ann can also attest: "Irv and I have each retained friends from our previous marriages. Others have fallen by the wayside, which I think probably would have happened even if we'd been in the old marriages." Some friendships are for life; others were right for specific times or places. While some may reflower, others were lovely while they lasted.

I like most of his friends, but some I don't have much in common with, and a few I don't like very much (I'm pretty sure they feel the same about me). Should I keep trying, for my boyfriend's sake?

You won't always like each other's friends, and this need not become an issue. If you tell your man tactfully that so-and-so is nice but you don't seem to have much in common, he'll likely be relieved he can tell you he feels the same about some of your friends! See those buddies when the other is busy with something else.

Now and then things get dicier. "When Andrew and I had dinner with Andrew's good friend Nick, we had a wonderful time," Faith told us. "So I was really looking forward to meeting Nick's wife. Boy, was I in for a surprise. She talked to Andrew and Nick as though I weren't at the table, didn't ask me anything about myself and barely acknowledged me throughout the entire dinner.

"I later learned she's best friends with Andrew's ex and tried hard to get them back together. Although Andrew and his ex had been split for a year before he met me, to her I was 'the other woman' and the breakup was my fault."

When a marriage ends, it ends for the couple's friends, too. There can be sadness, anger and taking sides. Know that it has nothing to do with you. Often these powerful emotions eventually lose momentum as people find ways to move on.

In the meantime, how you respond is always up to you. "Charlie's ex went around saying we'd been carrying on for years and that he left her for me. It drove me nuts and I felt embarrassed when meeting Charlie's friends. When I told a friend about this, she said, 'My husband's ex did that, too.' 'Doesn't that make you crazy?' I asked. 'No,' she said. 'If that's what they want to think, let them think it.' It was a good reminder that with the maturity of years it gets easier to take others' opinions less personally—and it's probably better for one's blood pressure!"

DON'T GET FAZED

If you just aren't clicking with some of his friends, do your best to connect as a grown-up, and if it doesn't happen, let it go. Pushing a situation usually just makes things worse.

Sometimes a rocky start to a relationship isn't about you at all. "Frank's best friend, Doug, was married to a woman who was extremely cool toward me, and I had no idea why," Keisha said. "In my twenties, her behavior would have thrown me, but since then I've learned that people just don't always get along. I didn't want to confront her and risk driving a wedge between Frank and Doug, so although it was uncomfortable, I never lost my cool. I think I became the master of the 'Hmm' and the 'Oh, really?' I also steered clear of being alone with her.

"But the story doesn't end there. A year later, she and Doug split up. I hadn't known that her marriage was in trouble, and I saw her behavior in a new light. I realized the last thing she'd needed back then was to be hanging out with her husband's incredibly happily remarried best friend and his new wife!

"Then something amazing happened. After I had my baby, I got a card from her! I responded. Suddenly we had a little connection going. We never became close friends, but she became much warmer.

We exchange holiday cards and chat at community events where we see each other. It's so much nicer than having to avoid her. The lessons for me were that you never know what's going on in someone else's life, and that this had nothing to do with me personally. To her I represented a spouse ending a marriage and moving on to find happiness, and that can be scary to people in a bumpy relationship."

What an inspiring example of a Garter Bride who paved the way to turning around a difficult relationship by choosing not to meet negativity with negativity! When the other person's ready, a happier ending may happen. And if it doesn't, you've kept your self-respect.

In the end, happiness can win hearts, as this Garter Bride discovered: "The first time I met Noah's friends was at a holiday party where I knew no one. I was nervous and spent hours planning my outfit and working on my hair and makeup. When we arrived, the hostess came up to me and said, 'It's great to see you. We've never seen Noah so happy and relaxed. We know you have everything to do with that.' At that point it didn't matter whether Noah's friends would become my friends, too, but being welcomed was a good start."

Going Pro: Office Parties, Schmoozing and Meeting the Boss

Sometimes even before you meet each other's friends or family, you meet each other's coworkers or business contacts, whether at the office holiday party or at a business social event.

First, two words on how much to say at work about your new love: be discreet. Once you feel fairly secure in your relationship, mention it casually. You want colleagues to see your relationship as part of your life, but not the main part when you're at work.

My boyfriend's company holds an annual party where employees can bring a guest. I'm sure his ex attended these. What kind of reception can I expect from his coworkers and their spouses?

"When we'd been dating about six months, Vic took me to the office holiday party," Helen told us. "He'd been at the firm for years, so they'd all met his ex. I could feel them watching my every move. What could be more fun for office gossip than a senior exec showing up with his girlfriend?"

Here's our advice for business/social events:

- **Remember to ask: "Anything I need to know?"** Don't wing it. Ask your boyfriend what he's told his colleagues about you, and what they thought of his ex-wife. You'll be more comfortable if you know what to expect.

- **Behave as if you're at work, just as you would at your own workplace.**

- **Limit public displays of affection.** What seems permissible to you may look inappropriate to someone else. It's fine to take his arm or for him to put his arm around you occasionally, but don't hang on each other all evening, nuzzle, whisper, kiss, sample each other's food or dance too close.

- **Avoid conversations about the ex.** Helen told us, "Vic's ex wasn't very popular, so people were receptive to me because apparently Vic was happier than they'd ever seen him. It was nice to hear them say things like that, but I was careful just to accept it graciously—just saying 'Thanks' or 'We're having a nice time together'—and then changing the subject. I didn't want things to slip into gossip mode."

- **Script the water-cooler conversation.** You want to be seen as a professional asset to each other. "I thought about what it would take for people to come up to Vic the next day and say, 'What a nice person.'" We think that's great advice from Helen. Imagine people talking about you around the proverbial water cooler. You want it to be only positive . . . and, frankly, kinda boring. "Hey, she's really nice" would be the perfect comment before they move on to what's going on with the World Series.

Meeting the Family: "Mom, Dad . . ."

Of the three of us, Ann takes first prize in the Who-Has-the-Most-In-Laws Sweepstakes: "Irv comes from an enormous family. The main branch lives in Philadelphia, and I first met them when Irv and I traveled there for a family birthday party. There are forty-four family members in the Philadelphia area, and on the train down I tried to memorize all those names! At the party, I occasionally matched a husband with someone else's wife, or married a sister to her brother, but they understood the confusion of meeting so many family members at once, and they didn't mind. Though at times it was confusing, I knew I was welcomed. Now when I can't sleep, I don't count sheep; I count Irv's family!"

"One of the many fun things about meeting your guy's family is looking at it as a way of making new friends," Tish adds. "When we'd been dating a year, John invited me to his family reunion in Maine. In my twenties I might have run for the hills, but in my thirties I'd been single for so long I got a kick out of big parties and I thought this could be a lot of fun.

"When I got there, I admit it was a bit overwhelming. There were kids running all over the place and I couldn't begin to tell who was who. I was standing on the porch in the 100-degree heat when I noticed a little girl lying under a heavy woolen blanket. Was she OK? Should I point this out to someone? Not having any kids of my own, I wasn't sure what to do.

"Then John's sister-in-law came up and handed me a glass of lemonade. We both looked down at the lumpy blanket and she said, 'Kids . . . they go through odd stages.' We both laughed. (John's niece emerged an hour later no worse for wear!)

"For the rest of the day John's sister-in-law took me around and introduced me to everyone, and since then she has become one of my closest friends. At the end of the day we all gathered for my first picture with John's extended family. When I look at it now and see John beside me and his big family around us, I know how lucky I am to have so many new people in my life."

It's almost stereotypical for younger couples to worry about getting along with each other's families. Younger women can get caught in the stressful role of go-between, trying to make sure everyone gets along. As a Garter Bride, you're comfortable with a more relaxed approach. Here are some strategies to keep in mind:

- **Remember what we said about larger versus smaller groups, and focal points?** In the Garter Brides' opinion, the right number for the first meeting lies somewhere between Ann's and Tish's experiences and close encounters with the folks. Together, figure out the right size for these meetings. And here again, focus on a shared activity helps.

- **Families, more than friends, may need time to warm up.** "Steve's family doesn't exclude people, but they're very close and it's hard to get into the inner circle," Claire recalls. "Steve and his sister adore each other, and although she was thrilled when we got together (she couldn't stand Steve's ex-wife), she had a hard time adjusting to the fact that our relationship took time away from her relationship with her brother. I had to give his family space but also give them attention—and time. They came around and we get along great now. But it took a while to crack the family code, so to speak."

Even if you all hit it off immediately, families don't always realize how their words or behaviors affect you. "Kyle's mother is the most charming woman who ever lived. After her husband died, I worked for days to help her clean out their house so she could move to a retirement home. While we were packing boxes, suddenly she handed me a photo album and said, 'Do you want this?' It was marked 'Kyle's First Wedding.' I had to wait a beat and remember that she felt so comfortable with me that she didn't realize I might not feel as she did about that album. So I chuckled and said, 'Thanks, Millie, but I don't think I'll be putting it on my coffee table.' I did take it home and gave it to my husband, so he could give it to his child."

■ *Whoever holds the power sets the tone.* There's generally one family member whom everyone, consciously or not, is trying to please, rebel against or circumvent. His or her reaction to you will likely be the "official" family view. "Neil's dad and I got along well, but Neil's mother was one of those take-over-the-room people, and she took a long time to warm up to me," Lydia told us. "I can't imagine her husband ever saying to her, 'Get a grip.' He should have, but he didn't."

Ideally, you and your boyfriend will talk about this before you meet each other's families, but if not, you'll probably figure it out by paying close attention during your first meetings. (Note: Sometimes the dominant person appears helpless or passive.)

■ *Do more listening than talking.* You can pick up important clues about the family dynamic by listening to their conversation. This will also help you find things to talk about. If there's a fun family tradition they engage in, that's a neutral but friendly topic you can introduce. Ann says, "Irv's mom always hosted a big Thanksgiving dinner at a restaurant on the Saturday after Thanksgiving.

Everyone went to their in-laws' on Thursday and to her dinner on Saturday. It was a lovely tradition, and had I been stuck for something to talk about during one of the first times we were all together, that's something I would have mentioned." Ask questions about their interests. Avoid political or religious discussions. Be open and relaxed, but don't bare your soul. Sound like first-date etiquette? Yup!

■ **Keep positive expectations.** These relationships can be wonderful. As Pat says, "Everyone's family is a little wacky, but we all think our family is the wackiest of all. I was probably more nervous than Mark about introducing him to my family. I shouldn't have been worried. My husband and my brother have become close friends. That's been a real bonus for me."

How much do first impressions count?

They count, but they're not irrevocable. We've all met people we liked better as we got to know them. And as a grown-up, you've seen how time and effort can change things—from ups and downs at work to friendships that go through periodic growing pains. If things get off to a shaky start, know that time is on your side. First meetings are stressful for everyone, and you'll all have do-over opportunities.

"I spent way too much time and energy feeling upset about my in-laws' bad behavior," one bride told us. "It took a while, but eventually our relationship became cordial, and even friendly. I learned things can start out one way and end in another that I never expected."

She's so right—and you've had many experiences in life to prove it. So trust in time and in what you already know about resolving tricky relationships.

Sometimes all it takes is one small act to warm a cool reception. "Shortly after Raphael and I became a couple, we went to a baseball game with his family. There was a lot of general conversation, but at some point I realized that his father had not said a word to me. I wasn't sure what to do, but finally I asked his opinion about some of the new players on the team. Once we started talking, things were OK. I think that showing him respect helped. I sought his opinion, and I made the first move."

Ultimately, if you're making their son or brother happy, you'll gain acceptance, which may come sooner than you think: "When Jonathan and I had been dating a few months (and we had a feeling it was going to lead to a wedding), I called his house one day and his sister, who was visiting, answered the phone. She told me how happy she was that Jonathan and I were seeing each other. It was wonderful to see him happy and 'whistling,' for which she credited my presence in his life. It made it so easy when I finally met her. I felt as though we were already friends (and we still are)."

If you hunkered down in your work during your single years, your newfound happiness may especially delight your families. When you're with someone you adore, you want to be out and about, showing each other off, sharing new experiences. Your joy is telegraphed to the people you're with. Said one bride: "Our families were so pleased—it was evident to them how happy we were. My brother-in-law remarked that I was so much more myself in front of my now-husband compared to previous boyfriends."

Our families seem more gun-shy about committing to our relationship than we were! What's going on?

"Once I became a parent," Pat says, "I understood the drive to protect one's child at all costs." In other words, families can do misguided things for good-hearted reasons. They may be slow to embrace your relationship because:

- They need to grieve the end of the previous relationship, even if ending it was for the best.

- They fear this is a rebound relationship that, if it leads to marriage, might end in another divorce and more hurt for their loved one.

- They sympathize with the ex if they loved the ex, and/or if they feel the ex was wronged.

- They're concerned for the welfare of any children involved.

- If both of you have children, his parents may be concerned that his kids will be shortchanged, since his kids probably will only see him on alternate weekends, and your kids will have far more time with their son.

To help address these issues:

- **Put it in perspective.** While the family's feelings are important, your primary relationship is with their son, and your first responsibility is to the two of you. Also, although your first response will likely be emotional, if you assess the situation objectively, you may recognize that you've dealt with some aspects of it before. "I spent some time just watching Kip's mom operate," said Janice. "And I realized she was a type that I knew—nice on the surface, but always judging. I found I could anticipate problems and sort of 'manage' her, the way I handle difficult people at work."

- **Seek the wisdom of your sisterhood.** Among your many girlfriends, someone's likely to have dealt with the personality or situation you're facing. Consult your trusted confidantes. You needn't go into detail about your circumstances. Just ask what their experience has been with difficult people and what they did about it. You may also consider seeking professional help for yourself or with your mate, to get a handle on the problem and learn some ways to manage it.

- **Remember you're in this relationship for the long term.** Rest in the security of your relationship. You can and will persevere.

- **Demonstrate your commitment.** In word and deed, show your goodwill and loyalty toward your mate and his family. This will reassure them that you take this relationship and its responsibilities seriously, and that you honor your mate's family ties regardless of their feelings about you.

For persistent or serious problems, here are some protective actions brides we know have taken:

- **Limit face time (boundaries, boundaries, boundaries!).** As a couple, agree on certain situations that are OK or not OK when those individuals are involved. For example:

  - An event where they're part of a larger group is OK, but one-on-one dinners are not.

  - When you visit, a long weekend is OK; longer than that is not.

  - Overnights at their house are not OK. "When we visited Arthur's parents, we'd stay at a local bed-and-breakfast," Michelle said. "They constantly pressed us to stay with them, but I held firm and had a response ready: 'Arthur works so hard that it's a treat for us to stay at the B&B—like a date. So we get to see you *and* have a nice date.' How could they say they didn't want their son to be happy and have a strong relationship? The B&B was our escape hatch. After dinner we'd go back there and relax. As a younger woman I'd have been too intimidated to hold my ground, but I had outgrown being Miss Perfect, caving to pressure to do the 'right thing'—which usually meant pleasing someone else."

- **Bring in the neutral.** By this we mean add a few others to the gathering whom you'll all be able to talk to, providing new faces and topics for conversation. "The first time we invited Derek's parents over for dinner, I invited our next-door neighbors to join us," Diana told us. "They're older than we are, but younger than Derek's parents, so they were a perfect generational bridge, and they're pleasant and easygoing. It worked beautifully. I did similar things for a long time afterward. It helped me relax and be myself."

- **Team up to do all you can to connect positively.** You should operate as a united front, together working out a strategy so no one is pushed to the point of saying "never again." It puts a person in a very difficult position to be told, for example, "I will not speak to your mother." We recommend making this effort because you don't want to force your partner to make an emotional choice between mate and family. Even if he, too, doesn't get along with his family, those ultimatums can put a wedge between you. As one Garter Bride astutely notes, "I wasn't going to be the one to drive him away from his parents, because I didn't want to be blamed if he felt guilty about it later. I think he might have been relieved, in a way, to have me as the excuse to break away from them. But it would have been very bad for our relationship."

As you talk things through, remember that your relationship and your feelings for each other come first. Even if you have different opinions, you can understand each other's position and seek creative ways to accommodate each other. For example, if his mother is very unpleasant to you despite all your efforts, he may need to see his mother on his own, while you see her only on major holidays when the whole family gathers. You can encourage him to include her as a regular part of his life without her being a regular part of yours. If the two of you are stumped for solutions, consider consulting a qualified therapist together to help you sort through the issues. Between you, you have decades of resourcefulness. Use them and don't let this become a point of tension between you.

Once you've set limits that make you more comfortable, it becomes easier to reach out in genuine ways. It's surprising how many options there are for communication. One bride told us, "I'd call or e-mail his parents with news about our lives. I'd mention I was reading about a subject they were interested in and ask their thoughts." If you're getting any points at all, you'll get points for effort—even if the effort looks hopelessly transparent to you.

- **Realize it may not be about you.** It's possible this would happen with anyone he went out with. Some families' dysfunctional behaviors are so entrenched that they aren't personal to *you*. We know it's hard to detach, but you should not let others control your happiness.

- **You don't have to love each other to get along.** Beth says, "My sister-in-law is not my type. But I think that she and my brother-in-law (also not my type) are a great couple and very well suited. In my twenties I'd have made Herculean efforts to be super-nice and have a close relationship. Now when we're together I'm civil and we even have some laughs. But I know that not all relationships work out, and that's OK."

In the end, what's most important is you and your man. Other relationships should only become a big deal if you and he fight about them. Whatever's between you and *them* should not come between you and *him*.

THE TRIPLE-DECKER SANDWICH GENERATION

The pressures of caring for elderly parents may come sooner and be more intense for the newly committed midlife couple, who may be simultaneously adjusting to being newlyweds (and possibly new parents and new stepparents) while also being caregivers to their own parents.

"Ritchie's parents and mine died within the first five years of our marriage, when our son was a baby," Alison told us. "My parents lived close by and I was glad I could be there for them, but it was tough combined with caring for my son. And it was sad, because I knew my son wouldn't remember them."

Make sure you and your man discuss in advance how you'll handle caregiving situations, since they're likely to happen sooner than later. If you have children and your parents are in reasonably good health, take that precious window of time to make extra memories together and keep a record—in the form of memory books, photographs, videos and other keepsakes—for you and your children to enjoy in later years.

I really like his parents—but his mother tells us what to do about practically everything. My boyfriend says that's just the way she is and that I should ignore it (he does). But her interference is driving me nuts. Any advice?

Many parents never seem to grow out of this. You can tactfully say, "Thank you for your thoughts/ideas/opinion." And that's it. "Soon after we married, my mother-in-law was telling me what to do about something or other," Ellen told us. "I could see it happening twenty years from now if I didn't nip it in the bud. So I very nicely, very quietly, said, 'You know, Deidre, I really respect your opinion. Please know, though, that the vote exists between Jordan and me.'"

This question brings up another issue girlfriends talk about: men who passively let their partners take care of the family relationships. As Garter Brides, we feel it's his job to set limits with his parents and your job to do it with yours. One of our brides is gently but firmly extricating herself from being the go-between: "I've had conversations with Jesse letting him know that I'm stepping back from some of the stuff I'd taken on as the 'girl's job'—especially relationships with his family. I've said, 'I want you to know that I'm adjusting my role, and I'm not going to handle everything anymore. A lot of great things have come from it, but it's taken a lot out of me. I need to renegotiate my role now.' When I was younger I would have gone along to get along. Now, if something's not working for me, I bring it up. If that upsets someone, I deal with it. I've learned not to take on family tasks I really don't want to do. And I can leave those situations as they are, even when they're not so great."

If you can sidestep these common pitfalls with each other's families, a wonderful opportunity opens up to connect grown-up to grown-up. For example, once his mother realizes you're going to politely but persistently ignore her advice on how to spend your money, raise the children, decorate your house and just about everything else, she may realize she has an opportunity to truly connect with another smart, can-do, grown-up woman in a world where women help each other best by sticking together. Ann fondly remembers Irv's mom: "She was a very smart, dynamic woman. Even in her last years she read two newspapers daily and pursued many interests. I sometimes kid Irv: 'Your mother was a much more interesting person than you.' He laughs and agrees. If I'd been in my twenties, I'd have found her intimidating. As an established woman with my own interests and accomplishments, I found her fascinating and loved spending time with her. I guess it's the confidence that comes with maturity." That confidence is your ace in the hole with your families.

Ex Marks the Spot

We wish *ex* had never become a word. There's a lot we could say about exes, both good and not so good. Some of our best friends are exes. Some of *us* are exes. So we aren't here to perpetuate negative stereotypes. No one gets married thinking they're going to get divorced, but we all make mistakes or go through changes, and ending a marriage doesn't always bring out the best in people. Here are some common questions and suggested strategies.

KEEP YOUR GIRLFRIENDS IN MIND

If all else fails in trying to keep your cool with an ex, visualize yourself telling your girlfriends later about how well you handled things—and then do that!

My boyfriend and I both have (and therefore are) exes. It's been rocky for all of us. Can there be peaceful coexistence?

We believe so, in all but the most difficult situations. Yes, there are exes who do unforgivable things: "Sean's ex pitted the children against him. He didn't even know his oldest son was engaged until he read it in the paper." Another bride told of her husband being excluded from his daughter's first communion: "He found out about it and went in quietly and sat in the last row, not talking to anyone because he didn't want to risk causing a scene. But he wasn't going to miss it." We've even heard stories where the police and lawyers had to be involved. If you are in a very tense situation with an ex—yours or his—don't hesitate to seek whatever professional help and security you need.

In more normal situations, it helps to bear in mind that ending a marriage and transitioning to a new life are rough on everyone, including exes. Here are some tools for making the process smoother:

- *Remember your man is with you now and wants to be with you.*

- *Fly above it.* Resist every impulse to get drawn into negativity—by the ex, by family and friends who are taking sides, even by your man. The husband of one woman we know is always bringing up his ex, although he's been married to our friend for a decade and was married to the ex for just a couple of years. It's like having the other woman in your marriage when there isn't one. Tell him to get over it!

- *Keep geographic distance.* It's possible even in small towns, especially since the ex is probably trying to do the same. "My friend Tess, her husband and his ex-wife all live on an island," Tamara says. "She told me his ex-wife doesn't use a certain path because she doesn't want to run into Tess."

- *Decide how much contact you need to have.* If children are involved, especially if they're young, you may periodically need to be in contact with the ex directly (see Chapter 4). Also know that you may have to guide your man in establishing boundaries for contact. One bride we know is dismayed that her husband's ex still calls him daily, even though their children are in college, so frequent communication isn't appropriate. His ex is hanging on to their relationship, and he still feels so guilty about the divorce that he's having a hard time setting limits. Our friend is working with her husband to wean his ex-wife off this pattern of behavior, as the time has come for her own feelings to be a priority.

NO BADMOUTHING—
AND WHAT TO SAY IF OTHERS DO

Others may say negative things to you about the ex. Responding in kind reflects poorly on you. As one bride notes: "Your ego loves it, but you can't be the one who continues that conversation. They feel it's OK for them to bring it up, but if you continue it, they may tell others you were badmouthing the ex! I just say something innocuous like 'Thank you' and then change the subject."

The badmouthing can sometimes be of your man. "Bryan and I were having dinner at the home of a couple he'd known for years. I was in the kitchen helping the wife clean up when she suddenly started talking about what an insensitive ass Bryan was in his previous marriage. At first I was speechless. Was she baiting me? Then I thought, everyone has to process the end of a relationship their own way. Maybe she was struggling. I'm a pretty honest, direct person and she was saying some things I knew about and agreed were bad behavior. So finally I said, 'Yes, he really didn't handle that well. Clearly they didn't bring out the best in each other. Things are different now.' It was a very politic way of saying that there's responsibility on both sides—and that it's over now. I think she was taken aback that I wasn't completely disagreeing with her."

We also like Ann's response: "I just say, 'I wouldn't know about that. Irv and I never talk about our former marriages—it doesn't help our relationship.' That's the truth, and it pretty much ends any gossip or negative talk."

Other positive deflectors:

- "I'm glad she's/he's happy."

- "We're very happy."

- "It was a difficult situation for everyone."

- "A lot of painful things happened for everyone, but things are moving to a better place now."

- "We're all working on making things better for everyone."

To Meet, or Not to Meet?

Geography and shared responsibilities generally dictate the level of contact with exes. If your man has kids, odds are high that at some point you'll meet their mother, perhaps at a graduation, major birthday, religious event, wedding or other milestone in a child's life.

TOP ETIQUETTE TIPS FOR EXES (IF YOU ARE ONE, OR KNOW ONE)

- Determine the best method for respectful communication. (What did people do before e-mail?)

- Be cordial to the new love in the ex's life.

- If the ex isn't with someone, remember that family gatherings or holidays are going to be much harder on the ex than on you. Kathleen told us: "Carlos and his ex have no relationship whatsoever, so when Carlos's son got married and we hosted a seated rehearsal dinner (the wedding was a buffet), I made sure Carlos's ex—who was coming without a date—was seated with members of her family and the bride and groom. I wanted to make sure that she was comfortable and therefore that the kids were comfortable."

- At command performances (school or religious events, graduations, weddings, funerals), nod or say hello.

- Do not vent to children at any time.

- Cultivate your love with your partner. Happiness is the best antidote to bitterness.

Olivia and her husband have shared custody of his two children. The children's mother lives in the same town, so the adults see each other all the time. It's not easy, but that's how it is and they all deal with it. As she says, "Grown-up pills aren't fun, but you have to take them. It's up to us as adults to make this work. The kids' comfort zone is a priority for all of us."

Sometimes there's just so much anger between exes that it's never going to work out; you'll never be one big happy family. Don't take it as your failing. And if your man explodes about how terrible his ex-wife is and rants and raves, soothe him and try to calm him down, but don't start agreeing or adding your two cents; just try to get the episode over with and move on.

WHEN IT'S "FORMER," NOT "EX"

If you or your boyfriend were widowed, many will delight in your newfound happiness, but some may need to work through grief and loss. Relationships with the deceased spouse's family can be tricky but can become warm and wonderful when handled with care. "My husband was widowed for four years before he met me. I invited his first wife's parents and siblings to the wedding—and they all came. I understood how difficult and generous it was of them to be there. It meant a lot to my husband. They still keep in touch, and I really like that."

When Arm's Length Would Be Too Close

Brides have shared positive ways to handle an ongoing negative relationship with the ex. One told us of an Internet-based service families can use to handle coparenting responsibilities, such as managing schedules and relaying information without having to contact each other directly or burden the children to function as intermediaries.

If you feel you can afford it, third parties can perform certain functions: "When my husband and I carried his ex on our health insurance, we hired a third party on a freelance basis to whom his ex could submit bills and insurance claims, so there'd be less contact. It didn't cost much and saved everyone a lot of angst."

If you don't already have telephone caller ID, consider it. "I can see when Phil's ex is calling and decide whether to answer or not. Generally, I don't. Their children are grown, so unless she indicates on a message that there's an emergency with them, I let Phil know that she called, and the ball's in his court to respond."

Positive attitude, patience and maturity are your allies as you and your mate combine your families and friends. Relish the good times that are surely in store, seek to strengthen bonds when that's needed and stay grown-up no matter what. You'll always be glad you did.

CHAPTER 4

"Nice Roast Beef, Honey, but Did I Mention My Daughter's a Vegetarian?"

Fitting Kids into the Picture

"I was turned on by Tony right from the start," Charlene said. "He was funny and charming, and he had sparkling blue eyes. Somewhere around dessert I took a deep breath and asked if he had any kids. He smiled and said he had five daughters. I felt this thud in my stomach and thought, *Five daughters? How can I get involved with this guy?* But I looked into those amazing blue eyes . . . and asked, 'Got pictures?' "

They were married two years later, with all five girls in the wedding party.

When you're over thirty-five and meet an eligible guy, there's a good chance he's already been married and has kids. Maybe that's true of you, too!

We speak of blended families from experience: We all married men who had kids (from very young to fully grown) and have six stepchildren among us. All of us are stepgrandmothers! If you're hoping to have a baby with this new man in your life, we've got that covered as well: Pat and Tish had children with their new husbands, as did many of the brides we interviewed.

It takes time and effort on everyone's part to make the new nuclear family work. But if you've heard or read stories that make the blended family sound like life in a Cuisinart, worry not. You'll be inspired and reassured by the road-tested resourcefulness and insights you'll find as our Garter Bride stepmoms talk about what worked (in one case, a whoopee cushion played a starring role!) and what didn't (attempting to do Thanksgiving the way the kids' mom did it) in becoming a stepfamily. In addition to ideas for building your relationship with your stepchildren, we'll share strategies for taking care of yourself. Combine these with your own wisdom, and you can feel confident that you'll be handling this important transition like a true grown-up.

GARTER BRIDE TIP

THE MOST IMPORTANT THING OF ALL

Remember you and his kids have a powerful thing in common: you all love him. You're not competing for his love. He loves you all, in different ways.

Getting the Timing Right

We both have children. When do we meet the kids?

Let's face it: all but the youngest kids know their single parents are dating. We don't suggest hiding your social life, but as we've said, we do advocate keeping the kids out of it until you feel it's important for them to enter the equation. While it might be more comfortable for *you* to combine love and parenthood, your children may not be ready for that step. "A friend of mine divorced when her daughter was about twelve," one Garter Bride told us. "Within a couple of years, my friend had guys spending the night. For an adolescent girl this was tough to take, and she moved in with her grandparents, who led a more conventional life."

"I never had anyone stay over when my daughter was at home," Bethany says. "That felt weird to me. When I first started dating, my daughter was upset about it, so I didn't have anyone pick me up at home. I felt there was no reason to upset her—especially when I was just dating and not seriously involved. There was even a man I dated for about a year who I didn't have stay over, because I knew he wasn't the one."

You can spend the night with each other when the kids are visiting their other parent. One bride called them "pockets of privacy." Like anything else in a grown-up life, you have to schedule it.

Bottom line: try to tailor your decisions about timing to the needs of the children involved, based on what is in their best interests. Every parent navigates this situation differently, and what worked for other people's kids might not be right for yours.

You probably already have a sense of what's appropriate from tuning into their age, temperament, how long you've been single and how they've handled the fact that you're dating. You won't go far wrong if your watchwords are *Put the children's feelings first.*

When do you tell the kids you're dating someone pretty seriously? It depends on your child's age and emotional maturity. Look for cues to your child's readiness. For example, watching a TV show together that features a single mother who's dating could be a conversation starter: "Gee, how would you feel if I went on a date?"

Put your toe in the water with a real-life example: "I just found out Aunt Mary has a boyfriend. Her son, [whom your child probably knows], thinks he's nice. They all had a picnic together. What would you think about doing stuff like that?" These conversations are often most effective when you're on a walk, in the car or in front of the TV. In other words, before introducing children to someone you're seriously involved with, introduce them to the *concept* of it.

Your kids' perceptiveness may surprise you. "After my first marriage ended, there was a seven-year period before I met Hugh, so my son, Cory, was used to the fact that I was dating. About six months into our relationship, Cory came into my room one night as I was getting ready to meet Hugh and said, 'Mom, he's a good guy. Don't screw this up.' That's when I knew it was going to work out. And it has."

GARTER BRIDE TIP

THERE'S NO RUSH

Let him know you're OK with not meeting his kids for a while and with keeping your interactions with them low-key, if he thinks that's best for them. Make it clear that it's important to you that his children's needs be put first. He'll be relieved you're helping him handle a touchy situation and showing sensitivity to those he loves.

Meeting the Kids

What's the best way to meet the kids and start to establish a relationship with them?

There are lots of ways to do this, as our brides' experiences show! Here's what they had to say:

- *Go slow and keep your expectations in check.* It would be unusual if you adored each other right away—so take a page from your experience with first dates: just get to know each other. It's true with grown kids, too: "When Stan and I got married, his daughter was nearly forty, and I didn't expect that we'd become the

Brady Bunch. I looked upon my soon-to-be stepdaughter and her husband as adults I hoped I would like and would like me."

- **Don't jump to "What happens if we get married?"** Another useful tactic is not to think too far ahead; just relax and enjoy yourself. One bride confided, "During that first meeting, I had a feeling I was the last person his kids wanted in their lives. A girlfriend told me the most important thing was not to try too hard, so I tried to keep my cool."

- **Shared fun is fun!** Consider going to a movie, where you can get a little acquainted beforehand, then talk about the movie afterward. Or maybe you all participate in a game where no one has to make conversation because there's stuff to do: hatching a strategy, tallying the score, cheering each other on. "Ted's kids were nine and thirteen and had been through a lot during his divorce. I was aware that getting to know them wasn't going to happen in one afternoon. I didn't want us to have a tense 'first date' in a restaurant. So we went mini-golfing and had fun."

- **Laughter is the best icebreaker.** One bride made the kids' dad the butt of the joke—literally! "When I first met Kerry's school-age kids, I brought a few small toys, gum and a whoopee cushion to the restaurant. When Kerry went to the bathroom, we put the whoopee cushion on his seat. The kids got a huge laugh out of it, and it created a fun atmosphere right off the bat."

- **Include people they know and like.** "Howard suggested we all meet at a restaurant for dinner with the couple who introduced us. Both sets of kids knew them, so they were comfortable, and it was a very easy meeting."

- **Keep it relatively brief and, if possible, an extension of something they're familiar with.** "I went to temple with my son and daughter—which is important family time for us—and I invited Ira to our house afterward to break the fast with some other family members, where the kids could talk to him a little or a lot. They liked him!"

- **Build on the positives.** One bride felt a strong enough bond after the first meeting to plan a more extended time together: "Several months later, we all went on a cruise together. It was a great way to get to know each other." This is a good example of how different things work for different people—and how you and your mate can use your grown-up good judgment to decide what to do.

HOW THEY MET THE KIDS

"I asked them questions about things they were interested in. They really liked cartoons, so I asked about their favorite characters and episodes. They talked for about an hour—it was a great icebreaker."

"I met his little boys a couple of months into the relationship. I took them out for ice cream and fell in love!"

Tish remembers, "John's kids were five and three when I first met them. I was a single working woman who knew nothing about kids, but somehow we made it through the first lunch. I ordered a sandwich; John ordered food for the kids and nothing for himself. I wasn't sure why he'd done that until the kids had eaten all they could and John ate the rest. That's when I knew I was in a whole new ball game!"

"When I first met my husband's two children, I said, 'You can call me whatever you like—you can call me Auntie, or you can call me Judy.' Whereupon the four-year-old said, 'Mommy calls you Bimbo!'"

continued

continued from last page

"Brian and I went to meet his son, Adam, at college. Adam brought two friends along, and I was glad he wanted his friends to meet us. Soon we were all having a great time, and everyone was laughing—when suddenly my temporary tooth implant fell out in my spaghetti! I tried to fish it out with a fork, but finally had to use my fingers. Adam and I still laugh about it."

"I met his daughter, who was in her twenties, after I'd been dating her dad for about a year. We spent the day skiing together. It went OK—not great, but not bad."

"I met Oliver's adult son at a family Thanksgiving dinner. I'd already met the rest of the family, which made things more comfortable. I felt shy around him, which was purely me—he was always very nice and seemed quite easy with me."

"Not that I was nervous or anything, but two hours before my step-daughter's plane was due to arrive for her first visit to our home, I spilled boiling water on my feet! I didn't want to cancel our scheduled visit to the museum. So we went (OK, I hobbled) and used a wheelchair that the museum provided. As she wheeled me onto the landing atop the museum's great marble staircase, we both looked at each other and started to laugh. 'I hope you're not having any hostile thoughts right now,' I said, 'because this is a great opportunity.' It was our first private joke."

"I travel sometimes for work and at one point was going to the city where Les's daughter, Amy, was living with her fiancé. She asked me to stay with them! Even though I preferred staying in a hotel, she insisted that I stay with her. We had a ball together and she told me I'd be invited to their wedding in a year. I said, 'I don't know if I'll be with your father then.' Amy said it didn't matter; they wanted me as their friend. One year later, I went to the wedding (with her father as my escort). I was seated next to the bride, and her mother was seated across the table. I knew then how much I meant to Amy."

What if my kids don't like him?

Most of the Garter Brides felt very strongly that their new relationship wouldn't have gone far if it hadn't worked for their children. Linda says, "As the mother of two very young girls, I was concerned about getting remarried. I was pleasantly surprised and comforted when I discovered how relaxed and in control Tom was with my kids, because he'd already raised two children of his own from his previous marriage. I also felt guilty that he'd have to deal with little ones—and eventually teenagers—all over again. But he convinced me that the kids and I were a package deal, and he was just fine with it."

When Nathalie met Max after a difficult divorce, she was gun-shy about getting involved with anyone again and was very protective of her three-year-old daughter. If a man wasn't going to be good to her daughter, it was a deal breaker. "One night the three of us went out to dinner. My daughter had stomach problems at the time and would vomit without warning. I went to the ladies' room and when I came back she had vomited all over Max. Max didn't flinch and was gently cleaning her up. That clinched it for me."

Allow for Emotional Adjustment

How can we help our kids get used to our new relationship?

Often a divorced parent's newfound love is difficult for children because many kids still fantasize that their parents will get back together. Being a mature bride is a plus, because you can understand how they must be feeling. "The kids' comfort zone is the priority for us," Betty says. "Decisions were made that changed their lives forever and they didn't have a vote." "My husband's teenage daughter lives with us part-time and I really like her," Phoebe says. "After her parents got divorced she moved around a lot, so I moved into my husband's house so that she didn't have to get used to yet another home. When she's older I look forward to moving to a place that I can feel is more my home, too, but right now it's important to put his child first."

It's also possible their other parent has been saying negative things about your relationship. One Garter Bride observed, "On some level they probably see having a relationship with you as a betrayal of their other parent." As another noted: "I bonded with my husband's grown son quickly because we both work in retail sales, so we had a lot in common. His daughter was more reserved out of loyalty to her mother, but I didn't push it, and slowly, over time, our relationship improved."

If a parent is deceased, the child may have a loyalty to the dead parent. This is a situation that requires especially sensitive handling. But this doesn't mean that all of you won't be able to develop a positive and caring relationship.

"Remember most second marriages are built on some kind of sadness, whether divorce or the death of a spouse," Rosanna says. "There will be sorrow woven into the joy." It's best to be compassionate and understanding, even if your overtures aren't at first reciprocated. Realizing that healing a rift between a child and a divorced parent can take time will keep you from getting caught in the no-win middle. "My husband's son is still angry with his father about the divorce and acts out frequently with him—not returning calls and so on," Anita says. "They have a lot of stuff to work out. I welcome him into our home and I support them both, but I'm careful not to interfere or try to manage their relationship."

Finally, give yourself time to regroup. One bride advises, "Give yourself credit for your successes—and take days off, as you would for your job." Another bride found it helpful to keep a journal about her feelings. This had an added benefit: when she read the entries later, she could see how her relationship with her stepchildren had deepened with time.

While connecting with stepchildren can be a delicate process, your good intentions have a lot of power. Tish recalls, "I just jumped into a whole new way of life. Love does that. I loved John, I loved his kids and together we had two more kids—and we had a responsibility to all of them. While I won't say we didn't hit some bumps, we were busy building the family I'd always wanted, and I knew we'd make it work."

When people who really care for each other get together, there's always the potential for happiness. "When a couple divorces, there is the end of a marriage, but also a reconfiguration of the family," Pat says. "In fact, if one or both parents remarry, the children have a shot at getting a 'bonus' parent. I hope my stepchildren see me as a bonus. They've been one for me. We're not the type of family we all may have grown up with, but we are a family."

Living the Blended Life

Now comes the next phase of the process: bringing the kids fully into your life together. Depending on the age of the children and the custody arrangements, that could mean full-time, part-time or visitation where the parent or the child travels to see the other. Tish remembers: "In the early years of our marriage, we lived in Boston, and John's children stayed with us on weekends. The house rocked with two preschoolers, two infants and two grown-ups. Then, when I got a job in New York, we moved to Connecticut to be somewhat equidistant from my job and John's children. I commuted on weekdays; he commuted to visit his children on weekends while I stayed with the two youngest kids. Sometimes he brought his children down from Boston. We held the speed record for changing the babies at highway pit stops. We'd do it in seconds and be back on the road. NASCAR had nothing on us! It was hectic, but it was also a blast. There's nothing more fascinating than watching children grow up."

"YOU'RE NOT MY MOTHER!" "HE'S NOT MY FATHER!"

Connie's stepdaughter didn't mince words: "You're not my mother. I already have a mother." Connie doesn't remember exactly how she responded, but she never forgot that emphatic statement. Even if you and your stepchildren like each other, they'll always have a mother who is not you, and of course you're not trying to replace her. What you can be is a caring adult in their lives who loves their dad and is trying to get to know them, too.

So take your cue for physical affection from them. They may not be ready for hugs from you, your parents and your relatives for a while.

Nor is your new mate your kids' father. "I made a huge mistake the first time we had both sets of kids together at Christmas," Barbara said. "Paul and I had been married about five months after dating for about two years. My first husband had died six years before and my daughters still worshipped him. Paul's son, daughter-in-law and grandchild were with us, and I said, 'I'm so glad we're a family.' Well, it was as though I'd poured ice water on my kids. I tried to talk to them afterward and they both kept saying it was OK, but I knew it wasn't. We were having a nice time and I'd pushed the envelope. I should have said, 'I'm so pleased we're all able to be together.'"

It's normal to make missteps now and then. It happens in every relationship, and stepfamilies are no exception. So go easy on yourself and trust that your relationship with each other's children will ripen with time. You'll do your best—and your best is very good. In the end, it's all right not to love your stepchildren. It's also all right if they (big breath here) don't love you, either. Your husband is the person you are spending the rest of your life with.

If you have children and your new husband has partial custody of his kids, on occasion try to make their stay with you happen at a time when your kids are visiting their dad or their grandparents. It's very hard for his children to know that your children have more access to their dad than they do. There are plenty of times when all of you will be together, but try to make time for his kids to be with just the two of you.

I'm walking on eggshells around his children. How do I keep it low-key (but not so low-key that they think I don't care), yet be involved without intruding?

Just like the first meeting, don't worry about everything going perfectly from the start. This is a long-term plan, so focus on forging a good, happy, loving and fulfilling relationship with your stepkids over time. One bride wisely counsels: "Let them get used to you without trying to win them over. Since I was a stranger to my stepchildren, I felt too much attention, gifts or questions would have been inappropriate. I just welcomed them like new friends. My role turned out to be that of a kind of 'aunt' position—more a friendly adviser than a parent."

Combining your lives may result in moments you'll be laughing about for years to come. Tish vividly remembers one of her first experiences as a brand-new stepmom: "One day John called down from upstairs and asked me to make the kids lunch, suggesting I just make them some baloney and cheese sandwiches. I went into the kitchen and panicked. What kind of bread? Mustard? Mayo? How many pieces of baloney? What kind of cheese? Twenty minutes later, John came down and asked the kids how they'd liked their lunch, but I was still trying to figure out how to make a kid's sandwich. Now I'm a baloney-sandwich-making whiz."

GARTER BRIDE TIP

NO LINES IN THE SAND, PLEASE

The important thing is not putting your husband in a position where he has to choose between you and his kids. That's a situation where no one wins.

Tune into What They Like and Watch for One-on-One Opportunities

Noticing and responding to kids' interests and preferences shows them you want to know them for who they are. "I began to ride bikes with my stepdaughter. I started paying real attention to her. One day she came home from school with a fruit juice container in her backpack that was a brand I'd never seen before. She told me she liked the juice they served in school better than what I had in the fridge. The next day I went out and bought that kind. It was a little thing, but it meant a lot: when she came home the next day and saw it, she smiled at me."

When the kids aren't at your home, phone and e-mail make it easy to stay tuned in: "I call to ask how tests and dates went. We invite them and their friends out to dinner with us and take an interest in their lives. I watch the movies they're into and some of the TV shows they're excited about, even though they might not interest me so much. I want them to feel I care about their lives and interests."

LET THE GOOD TIMES ROLL?

You never know when you'll turn the corner with a stepchild. Often it's not when you expect. Krista remembers meeting Jed's ten-year-old son, Scott, at a big amusement park. "There was this huge Tower of Terror ride that scared me to death. Those kinds of rides are my nightmare. But there I was with Scott begging me to go on it with him because it would be 'so much fun.' Yeah, right. But I thought, *He's got to be feeling at least some hostility toward me,* so I said, 'Let's go.' Well, we did. Four times. It was every stepkid's fantasy: a terrified, screaming, nauseous stepmom who was having a bad hair day. But what I discovered was that it was the first time that Scott and I really made a connection. We began to have our own relationship, our own history together that was just about us, not about him and his dad. It was a good start. Now I say, 'Scott, honey, do you even *know* how scared I was?'"

With adult children, having a simple thing in common can be a connection to build on: "My stepdaughter's a huge movie buff and so am I. I think we've both memorized every movie from the 1930s on. Talking about film trivia kick-started our friendship. Now her father says, 'You know more about what's happening in her life than I do.'"

If you don't have kids, don't let that keep you from reaching out. One bride says: "I let my uncertainty about how to relate to kids hold me back from my stepchildren. There's a fine line between not intruding and trying to get too close too fast, but I stayed a little too removed from them. I think I should have been more involved with them earlier than I was."

To that end, watch for times when you can be alone with your stepkids in casual-but-fun ways, whether it's just running errands with a stop for pizza, a little shopping trip or an outing you know they'll enjoy. "I took each girl out by myself, doing things I knew they'd like. Just the two of us—no husband. It built a bond between us and showed that I liked them as individuals—not that I just did stuff with them because they were visiting their dad."

You can do the same with grown stepchildren: "My grown stepdaughter moved in with us temporarily and was unfamiliar with our city's public transportation system. Early on in her stay I took her out for a Mexican lunch and then on a tour of the Metro routes I thought she'd be most likely to use. She felt more secure traveling alone after that and it was a perfect way for the two of us to connect on our own."

Agree as a Couple on House Rules

When his kids are at our house, I think my house rules should apply. But when I try to enforce them, things get tense! I realize the transition between houses is tough on them, but how do I get a say in my own home?

Work on establishing a set of operating principles that all of you can (more or less!) live with. If possible, you and your man should try to agree on how things such as discipline, homework and friends are handled at both your house and their mother's house so there's some sense of continuity. Two wildly different sets of rules is confusing for everyone.

TAKE A TIME OUT—FOR YOU!

You might not have as much patience with each other's kids as you have with your own. A word to the wise: if you feel driven to the edge, hang on to your temper and give yourself a time-out. Step back and say, "I need some time to think this over." It's good for you, and a great example for the kids! Call a friend and vent if you want to. Most of us have been on the receiving end of temper explosions at one time or another and know from experience they never help and are rarely forgotten.

It may not happen overnight, so everyone needs to be patient and tactful, especially since criticizing the kids' behavior can come across as criticizing the parent's parenting. "When his kids visited, they wouldn't even pick up a plate from the table," Etta recalls. "When I first spoke to Bobby about this, he felt his kids were being criticized. I brought it up again at a more neutral time, and he agreed to make some changes and suggestions when his kids were there."

Many brides shared how in time they worked out solutions with their stepkids directly. Susan remembers being dismayed when Charlie's daughters, ages ten and twelve, came to spend the weekend and did nothing to help around the house: "After unsuccessfully trying to get their dad to say something to them about it, I told them it would mean a lot to me if they helped out. It didn't happen right away, but as the weekends went on, they started to do a few things and it got easier for me to ask for their help. I'd been so afraid of being the 'wicked stepmom' that I hadn't wanted to rock the boat."

All children (step- or not!) generally need some fine-tuning in the "house rules" department at some point. Brenda was in her early forties when she married for the first time. "Glen's seventeen-year-old son, Connor, and I got to know and like each other quickly, but it was my first experience with children. I had a full-time job and Glen was on the road a lot for his job. When he was away I'd come home, put on PJs, grab a bowl of cereal and spend the evening happily being a couch potato. Well, Connor, who lived a few blocks away, got into the habit of dropping in with his friends, taking over the living room, raiding the fridge and monopolizing the TV.

"I tried hard to be pleasant, but my privacy was being invaded and eventually I was doing a slow boil. When I turned to Glen for help, he said, 'It's his home, too.'

"One night the kids pulled out cigarettes, and then I really did let them have it about not smoking. Glen would have had a fit. The next day I asked Connor to come over that evening alone. I told him that this was his home but that he had to respect the way I lived, which was about a lot more than not smoking, and that there would be other new rules. For example, he could come over as often as he wanted, but I asked him to phone first if he was bringing friends; if I was tired, I'd be in my bedroom with the door closed and he shouldn't take it personally; and if I wanted to use the kitchen or living room while he was here, we would have to share it in a reasonable way.

"That conversation changed our dynamic for the better. I think Connor appreciated that I dealt with him as a grown-up (and that I never told his father about the cigarettes). It could have had a terrible ending, because I was so close to blowing up, but thank goodness I found a way to state my boundaries calmly; otherwise our lives would have forever changed."

Most kids eventually grow into their roles as responsible house-mates: "My stepdaughter will often set the table and will do her laun-dry (which I taught her to do)—especially when she wants to wear something that's in the hamper!"

Be a Good Sport . . . but Be Yourself

You want your stepkids to like *you*. As one Garter Bride said, "If you present yourself as someone you're not, you'll never be able to keep it up over time. You are who you are, which is why the man in your life loves you in the first place. That's the woman he wants his kids to meet."

So be tactfully honest early when things affect you. "I wanted the kids to like me so much that I let them get away with any-thing for a long time. Then it was hard to express my opinions and enforce them. When I finally did, everyone was shocked. I wish I'd said what I'd thought earlier on. It's more honest and creates a truly loving and open atmosphere. Kids are adaptable, and I should have been more confident that I could keep their love even when we disagreed."

Besides, as one bride noted, "It's obvious when you're trying too hard." Tish adds, "You need to be able to express yourself about all that is going on, but you want to be sensitive about how your comments will be heard by everyone in your new family."

Risk being vulnerable by telling them about your mistakes—this, too, shows them who you are and helps forge a bond. "I've told the kids tons of stories about my failures and embarrassments. I want to help them see that it's OK to make mistakes and admit to them. It has brought us closer and allowed them to truly know me, maybe even better than some of my coworkers and friends. Now some of my more hilarious past moments are oft-retold legends! These 'Remember when you . . .' stories also remind me not to take myself so seriously."

NEVER SAY NEGATIVE THINGS TO THE CHILDREN ABOUT THEIR PARENTS

One bride told us, "I made a huge mistake about that. One day my husband went to pick up his thirteen-year-old daughter, Brittany, and she and her mom got into some kind of big fight before she got into the car. Brittany walked into our apartment, slammed the door and said, "My mother's a *witch!*" Without even thinking, I said, "You're right!" The whole room went quiet. My husband froze, and I'll never forget the look on Brittany's face. It took us all a long time to put that behind us. I never made that mistake again."

Set a Good Ex-ample

Whether it's kids commuting between households or your mate traveling to visit them, stepfamilies often are moving between two worlds—one of which contains the ex.

If your husband and his ex-wife need to see each other regularly for weekend pickups and drop-offs, parent-teacher conferences, sports events and so on, then you will probably see her, too. You also may get the "Jimmy left his history book at your house" messages, the "Why did you let him stay up so late?" rants, or the "She gets three doses a day, with meals" calls. Be clear about letting your husband know your comfort level about having contact with his kids' mom. It's up to him to take the lead with his ex. In these days of e-mail, cell phones, faxes and scanned documents, they have many options for handling logistics and paperwork (such as tuition or medical bills) without your having to be involved.

Make a plan together for how you'll handle this and keep revising it until it works. It's important that the grown-ups work to make these transitions as smooth as possible for the children. One thing everyone can agree on: battlegrounds aren't good places to raise kids. "I was fifteen when my parents divorced, and it was a long, messy, emotional process," Polly told us. "My mom bitterly blamed the woman my dad soon married for everything that happened, and I didn't speak to my stepmother for years. Having lived in a situation where the kids absorb their parents' anger, I try hard to keep any problems the adults are having with each other away from the children."

Here's how some other Garter Brides handled this issue:

- "I don't interact with the kids' mother; my husband does, and if their mother is going to be at the kids' school events, I don't attend. I think the kids are more comfortable when it's just their parents— not their dad with his wife and their mom with her boyfriend."

- "We only see my husband's ex at family events. We don't speak unless we have to, but we're very civil."

- "Although we don't initiate socializing with the kids' mother, we're fine when we're jointly included at events."

- "When my husband's daughters graduated from high school, I made photo albums of them and their mom and sent copies to her. I felt good about behaving in a thoughtful manner, staying true to who I am."

- "My husband's ex-wife has been phenomenal. She has made it extremely easy for me to develop a relationship with and love her daughter—and let her daughter love me."

- "I'm sure I'll never be able to tell her this, but I'm grateful to my husband's ex-wife for not turning her children against ours. If our kids didn't speak to each other, it would have killed my husband and could have torn my family apart."

THERE'S A BOND THERE

"I never forget that my husband and his ex-wife had these kids together. The bond they have from that will never change. Greg's ex-wife came to his mom's funeral. When I saw her there, I realized she, too, had a relationship with his mom, who was her children's grandmother. There will be graduations, showers, weddings, christenings, bar mitzvahs and lots of other family gatherings in the future. As grown-ups, it's up to us to make sure things go as smoothly as possible."

■ "My husband's ex-wife is pretty amazing. We all go out to eat or have dinner at our house a couple of times a month. Even though she must have had some mixed feelings, she has never shown animosity. It's a great situation—although the kids keep suggesting we all live together!"

Practice Wise Involvement

Children may disagree with their parents for any number of reasons, but stepkids' feelings about their situation can add an extra dimension to these encounters. What's a stepparent's role here? Using your grown-up smarts to practice what we call "wise involvement" can help chart a course. Sometimes your coaching from the sidelines may help everyone be more objective.

IF THE PARENT RELATIONSHIP WORKS, SO DOES THE STEPPARENT RELATIONSHIP— JUST DO THE BEST YOU CAN

If your man and his kids are close, chances are you can get close to them, too. If their relationship is strained, it may be difficult for you to get to know them. Do the best you can in helping your husband patch things up with his children, but remember that you're not responsible for problems that existed before you came along.

We know of times when a bride's wise involvement helped heal the parent–child relationship. Kathy remembers: "Sam's son Tim was really angry at him about Sam's divorce. Often Sam would fly to visit him and Tim wouldn't be home or would cancel the plans, and he never visited us. It was so painful for Sam that he sometimes talked about giving up on visits and just sending checks. I'd say, 'You have to go, otherwise it will just confirm Tim's beliefs about you.'

"Then Tim got his driver's license. He was dying for a car. And he expected his father would buy him one. It was Sam's opportunity to truly parent his son.

"He wrote Tim a letter that basically said, 'My role as your father is to teach you how to be in the world, to teach you about relationships. Relationships aren't one-way streets. You can't treat me with disrespect, not take my calls, not visit yet expect a huge gift. Relationships don't work that way. If you want a car, treat me with respect.' Tim tried to bargain, but Sam insisted on meaningful contact. Tim ended up waiting a year for a car—which seems like forever in the life of a teenager.

But it was a turning point in their relationship. Instead of losing his son by setting limits, as Sam had feared, now they talk nearly every day."

Even adult kids and their parents sometimes need the path smoothed by a wise stepmom. "When Buddy's ex-wife died unexpectedly, I said to him, 'You've got to go to Chicago to help your kids. Yes, they're grown, but it's the first death they've had to deal with and they're going to need help.' The divorce had been extremely acrimonious. There had been absolutely no relationship between my husband and his ex-wife for years. Still, we both knew it was essential that he help his kids during this time. He went, assisted them in making the funeral arrangements and flew home. We both felt it was the right thing to do."

Step Out of the Middle

Sometimes the best way to help your husband and his kids work out their issues is by stepping back. Pat notes, "There's a balance between being involved and being too involved." As Becky humorously told us: "In certain matters, mind your own business! I used to tell my husband how to parent—even though I wasn't a parent myself! I learned that in matters of kids' education, money/allowance, schooling and other sensitive issues, putting in my two cents just created problems. After all, they are his kids." And Ann says, "I may voice my opinion, but I don't offer advice! And there's a big difference."

Emma, who had a very good relationship with her own stepmother, recalls, "My stepmother was always present without being intrusive." She has taken that same style and used it successfully.

Gayle says, "When my stepdaughter visits, I make sure she and her dad have time for a walk by themselves or to go out for a cup of coffee. I encourage him to send her funny cards and to call her when I'm not around so she knows he's calling on his own initiative."

Nadine encourages Carl to have dinner or lunch with his kids as often as he can and she stays home. "When the kids call, I'm always careful to get their dad for them right away and I never chime in on the extension phone. They need to keep their relationship strong and it means a lot to all of them."

His children confide in me, which puts me in a weird position. I'm flattered they like and trust me, but I don't want to run interference with their father or keep things from him. What's your suggestion?

Jessica hit it off right away with Brett's daughter, Wendy, who was two when Brett got divorced. When Jessica and Brett got married, Wendy, then sixteen, began spending more and more time with them. One day she told Jessica she had a serious boyfriend she was crazy about. Clearly it was time for Wendy to see a gynecologist to find out about birth control. Brett spoke to Wendy's mom about it and she told him there was no way she was going to take her daughter to find out about birth control. If Jessica wanted to take her, fine.

So Jessica called for the appointment. "There I was, sitting in the waiting room with Wendy, and all I could think of was: *Could I have done this if Wendy were my daughter? I don't think so.* But Wendy had come to me—not her dad or her mom—to tell me about her boyfriend, and that meant a lot to me. I wanted to help her, and I was glad I could."

Sometimes when you're a stepmom, you're trying so hard to get your stepchildren to like you that it's easy to forget that at the end of the day kids will be kids. One bride remembers, "One day when Jay went to pick up his daughter Emily, she announced to him she was going to get her hair dyed pink and that her mother had said it was OK. Then she asked if I would take her. I was so thrilled that she actually wanted *me* to take her *anywhere* that I jumped at the chance. When we got to the salon, I settled in to read a magazine, and the next thing I knew Emily was at the door, ready to leave—with the same short brown hair she'd always had. On the way home, she told me that her mother hadn't said it was OK to get her hair dyed pink. She'd just thought if she had it *done,* it would be too late to change it. When we got home, Jay stopped in his tracks when he saw her without the promised pink hair. I just shot him a look that said, *Don't say anything.* After that, we learned to check with Emily's mom ourselves just to make sure everyone was in agreement as to the plans."

If your stepkids confide in you, how do you steer a responsible path without betraying their trust? Here's how Penny did it: "I became friends with my husband's teenage kids to the point that they'd call me for all sorts of advice and admissions of guilt, extracting promises not to tell their dad, my husband. This was easy for some things, but hard for others that I felt could be endangering them somehow. Sometimes I had to tell their dad, out of a sense of responsibility. But that made me feel like a traitor to the kids. On the other hand, I didn't want to keep something from my spouse that I shouldn't. Recently when that happened with one of the kids, I invited her to tell her dad. I said I was confident that her dad wouldn't punish her if she was truthful about it. I offered to talk to her dad and prep him first. This solution worked really well. She told her dad what she'd done, and while my husband was upset, ultimately he was proud that she'd been honest. And it worked out for me, too, because I hadn't allowed myself to be stuck in the middle of keeping a secret or spilling one."

When these relationships work as they should, there's a beautiful opportunity to offer stepchildren your perspectives as a caring adult member of their family. What could be better parenting than that?

Remember, Babies Can Build Bridges

We both have children, and we want to have kids together. Any advice?

Lily was thirty-seven when she married Joe, who was forty-five. "My husband had a married daughter. She became pregnant at the same time I did. I was extremely concerned that our simultaneous pregnancies would be difficult for my stepdaughter, but then a friend said to me, 'Remember, babies build bridges.'" And so they do, because they're important to everyone in the family.

Sometimes kids worry that if the two of you have more children, those children will be more important to you than they are. Tish remembers, "When I got pregnant the first time, I was on pins and needles about telling John's kids. He decided to announce the big news the next time he went to pick them up. They were a little late getting back, and—this was before the days of cell phones—I started to worry. Were his kids upset about the baby? Then I looked out the window and saw his car pull up. His daughter jumped out carrying a bouquet tied with a pink ribbon and with a card that said, 'I hope it's a girl!' His son jumped out with a bouquet tied with a blue ribbon and with a card that said, 'I hope it's a boy!' It was one of the most wonderful moments of my life, and it made me realize that the most important thing we needed to do was to let John's kids know that they were here first and we would always be there for them. By doing that, they would feel secure enough to welcome their new baby brother or sister—and they did."

Shannon remembers when Adrian's oldest son and his wife had a baby: "Adrian and I went to the hospital to see them. There was Bridget, this adorable little baby girl who looked at us all with these big round blue eyes, and I suddenly realized that she didn't have any idea who was who. All she knew was that there were all these people around who loved her. When I held her for the first time, and when my kids held her, I felt like the circle had been completed. We were a family, however complicated. It felt great."

Pat says, "I became a mother at forty-four—the same year my stepdaughter had a child, so I became a mother and a stepgrandmother in the same year! Becoming moms at the same time gave my stepdaughter and me a whole new way to connect. It provided much more than a neutral playing field—it gave us a happy one."

Know That Time Is on Your Side

Time ripens relationships. Rebellious teenagers grow up, become young adults, get married and have babies that bring added joy. "Something that's making you crazy now will pass because things do change. During the first years of our marriage, Lawrence's girls were constantly calling him, dropping by without notice and bringing friends over for meals without letting me know in advance. But after a few years, they graduated from college and went off on their own, and now we both wish we saw more of them. Things like that change over time. That's how life is. I know that now, but I didn't know it then."

Abbie had three kids and had been divorced for only six months when she met Gus. He had two daughters who were eighteen and twenty at the time and her kids were eight, eleven and thirteen. She worried about meeting his kids. What if she didn't like them? What if they didn't like her? And what if her kids didn't like his kids?

Well, as it turns out, she didn't really like his daughters. They were very close to their mother and were wary of Abbie. Her kids didn't like them, either. For a while, she and Gus weren't sure what to do. If they got married and moved her three kids into his house, how were all of them going to live together?

What happened was something she hadn't expected. "As it turned out, by the time Gus and I got married, one of his daughters had gone to college and the other was a senior in high school. In the year that it took my kids to adjust to a new home, a new stepdad and new schools, his daughters were both in college. When they came home for weekends and vacations, it was crazy, chaotic—and a lot of fun! The younger kids looked forward to having 'older sisters' at home, and I did, too. The older they got, the easier they were to be with. And having them around made my husband so happy—which meant a lot to me.

"Something else nice happened. Before I knew it, his daughters got married, and I had two wonderful sons-in-law who had no history with all that had gone on years before." Once again, time made all the difference.

And if his kids don't like yours, as one bride says, "Keep neutral. Don't get emotional when you discuss this with your guy. Try to keep cool; it'll be easier for him, too. And he'll take his cue from you."

Build Your Love

"Always make time just for you and your husband, even if it's only a weekend," Renée advises. "Your marriage is the reason everything else is going on, and you have to keep that strong. I actually love my husband more now than the day we got married." She should know: between them, she and her husband have seven children!

A few brides admitted feeling jealous of their mate's relationship with his children. But remember when he chose you, he took a big risk with his kids in order to have you in his life. When all's said and done, your marriage is where you can have the greatest positive influence—on the family's happiness as well as your own. "My stepdaughter grew up in a household where there was a lot of shouting. I think it's been very good for her to see a happy marriage. She knows I've made her father very happy, and I think that has made my stepdaughter happy."

When kids have been through a divorce, what they really don't need is to go through another one. Keeping your marriage strong is the best gift you can give them.

GARTER BRIDE TIP

RELAX AND RECHARGE

Everyone needs a break sometimes—so be sure to give time to yourself. Here's how some of our Garter Brides did it:

Always remain close to your girlfriends. Have "chick nights" where you go out and just have fun. If you feel really stressed, have a sleepover with one of them or get away for a weekend of R&R.

Keep a journal of your experiences and feelings. Not only is this reflective, private time good for you, but as mentioned earlier, it can help you recognize your progress as a stepfamily.

Read pertinent books and get counseling if you feel it could be helpful. Sometimes we need an empathetic and objective third party to help us get a handle on situations and coach us through them.

Remember your husband asked you to marry *him* . . . not his family.

How Do You Know When It's Working?

When stepfamily relationships work, they are deeply rewarding. "My son was a year old when my ex and I split up. When my son was five,

I had been dating Don for about two years and we had decided to get married. Don was all prepared to tell him. He told my son he could call him Don or Uncle Don, or they could make up a special name for him that just the two of them would use. My son gave Don a wonderful smile and said, 'Daddy.'"

There are lots of subtler signs, too, including your own increasing level of comfort and ease. We find when you start to notice normal family stuff emerging, it's a sign that everyone is relaxing around each other. Nancy was unsure of her relationship with her stepdaughter, who is seven years older than Nancy's son, Chris. Chris was lobbying hard to have his own website and was getting nowhere fast with his mother. Nancy found out that Chris was e-mailing his stepsister and asking for advice on how to handle this. "When I saw my son and step-daughter interacting as siblings, I knew then that all the normal family stuff was happening in its own time. That felt great."

HOW THEY KNEW IT WAS WORKING

"About a month ago, I kissed Sara for the first time. I was putting her to bed and I kissed her on the forehead. She seemed pleased. It was a big step for her—and me."

"One time when I was in the car with the kids and a few of their friends, I overheard one of the friends ask one of my stepdaughters if it was weird having another mom. 'No,' she said. 'There's just more people.'"

"When Liza got engaged, she told me she wanted me to be a part of her wedding, which meant a lot to me."

"A friend of my stepdaughter's told me that my stepdaughter is crazy about me. This was great to hear from an outside source, because my stepdaughter is not very demonstrative."

Take a Creative Approach to Holidays and Traditions

Holidays, birthdays and other special occasions are complicated. If the kids are with us, the ex is alone—and vice versa. The traditions the kids are used to aren't the same anymore, either. How can we make holidays work for everyone?

In every family, special occasions—holidays, birthdays, weddings and the like—are filled with joy, fun, wonder and sometimes complexity between families' busy schedules and changes evolving as kids grow up. Stepfamilies face these issues, too, with more of everything: "The most difficult thing in the world is to get all of us in the same room at the same time!" says Tish.

Combining creativity with grown-up common sense, our Garter Brides have found wonderful ways to mark special occasions in busy blended families. Ann and Irv host a Christmas banquet at a Chinese restaurant: "The invitation's open to our family and friends who are available to join us; it's become a tradition that's grown over the years. We now number over forty people! We all feast and have a great time, and no one has to cook or clean up."

One couple with seven grown children between them has a Sunday dinner tradition with "reverse reservations"—you call if you can't come; otherwise, you just show up! They cook up a storm and with the kids, spouses, boyfriends and grandchildren, every Sunday is an ever-changing family reunion. Personally, we think blending traditions and creating your own are great excuses to have more parties!

Here are some other examples of how brides handled this:

- "We've worked out holidays well with our exes. On Thanksgiving my husband's kids come to us and my kids go to their father.

The following holiday, we reverse it. That way we always have some family with us on holidays and the kids don't feel they've abandoned their other parent!"

- "I'm Jewish and Mario is Catholic, and combining our holidays has enriched our lives. I'd never had a Christmas celebration before, so it's fun for me to celebrate with Mario and his kids. He'd never been to a Passover Seder, so experiencing that is great for him."

- "As the kids have grown up, we've all had to become more flexible because we're all busy. The kids now have families, jobs and limited vacation time. My stepkids spend Thanksgiving and Christmas with their mom because otherwise she'd be alone. As the daughter of a divorced mom, I understand that. So we've made holidays flexible. A birthday doesn't have to be celebrated on the actual day. Thanksgiving might be on Saturday, when the kids can come to us. Everybody tries to make it work."

- "When the kids were young, Harvey and I created theme dinners—Greek Night, Mexican Extravaganza, Italian Abbondanza. I made quirky, funny invitations, and Harvey and I made food and played music that fit the category. It felt special—like a holiday. It also built some new and different family memories and reminded them that we were fun!"

Lucy smiled as she told us this story: "I'll never forget after the baptism of my stepgranddaughter, my husband and I got in the car with our young adopted son and I asked my husband, 'So, honey, how do you feel? What's it like to sit in a church with your Jewish wife, your ex-wife sitting next to you, your Korean son on your lap and your Catholic granddaughter being christened?' He put his head on the steering wheel and said, 'Oh my God, I have such a headache!'"

Life in a stepfamily is never dull! But as one bride told us, "I get angry when people refer to my stepchildren as 'baggage.' To me they're a bonus. I feel lucky to have them in my life."

So many brides shared how much these bonus relationships mean to them. One bride told us, "It hasn't been easy, but it has been very much worth it. I love my husband and I have a full and happy home— one that gives me great comfort. I didn't have that in my first marriage." Another one said, "My household is barely controlled chaos, but there is *so* much love in this house. If I hadn't gotten married again, I'd be working late every night, going home to a frozen dinner. That was not the life I wanted. On the holidays, the house is full of kids, the dog, Walt, me and my family, and I look around and think, *Could I have a pristine place and work weekends? Sure . . . but I'm grateful I don't.* I also have a man who loves me, who brings me flowers, who touches me—I know all of this is worth it."

As moms and stepmoms ourselves, we couldn't agree more.

CHAPTER 5
"Your Couch or Mine?"
Moving In Together: Romance and Reality

"You have *three* couches, lady," the moving man said to Tish in awed tones.

Actually, it was two couches and a loveseat. And what did you expect when two grown-ups set up housekeeping? As Tish says, "When you move in together at twenty-one, your stuff fits in a Volkswagen Bug. At forty-one, it's a seven-passenger van."

But who cares when congratulations are in order! There's nothing more exciting than planning your future. And making a home together is the joyful expression of that.

NESTING NOTES

Ann remembers, "When Irv and I got married, we discovered how much fun it was doing the ordinary things you do every day with someone you love. Sunday mornings we curl up and read the papers together, we often put on music and dance, and we're both hooked on good mystery stories. There are so many wonderful, simple, touching things about living each day with someone you love."

Taking the Leap!

We're thrilled to be moving in together, but there's so much to think about: where to live, how to combine our households and lives—plus we have our kids to consider. What should we be aware of before we take this big step?

Isn't it great to have another person to work this stuff out with? As Garter Brides, we can tell you that whatever you set your minds to as a couple, you can do. "There's a myth that when you're older you're set in your ways," Pat says, "yet everyone I know who fell in love later in life made real changes and did it happily. I was more flexible when I married at thirty-nine than I would have been at twenty-five! Being in love and having a happy home come first. I'm clearer now about the things that are important to me, which simplifies working things out."

Ann says, "When I was younger, I tended to define myself by what the other person wanted. Now what defines me are my relationships and the overall quality of our life together. With Irv and me, it's about considering each other's needs. We look at things and say, 'Whom is this more important to?'"

Here are some key things for the two of you to talk over before you begin loading the moving van.

Is He the First Person You'd Like to See Every Morning?

The right time for moving in together is very personal. You'll feel when you want the deeper connection of sharing physical space and daily life with the man you love—including making decisions, participating in each other's work and social lives and bringing together your personalities, habits and lifestyles. You're less likely to bow to social pressures and can let your relationship grow in its own time, as you both want it to.

NESTING NOTES

"I think the advantage of being in a mature relationship is that you don't have as many preconceived ideas about what it's supposed to be. You have enough life experience to know it's what you both need and agree it to be."

Check Divorce and Child Custody Agreements

Before you move in together, it's important to check your divorce and custody agreements to see whether there might be any stipulations that should be included as part of your planning process. Look for provisions that previously weren't applicable to your situation or didn't seem particularly important when the documents were drawn up.

One woman's divorce decree stated that she could have a partner move into her home for up to thirty days; after that, she would lose her alimony. When she'd agreed to those terms, she'd thought she'd never get involved with a man again. Two years later, she felt differently.

Another woman's ex-husband took her to court to stop paying alimony when she moved in with her boyfriend, on the grounds that he was paying to support her, not her and a guy. (He won the case!)

If children are involved and the other parent's permission is necessary to move a child to a different school district or city, your moving might be prohibited altogether. "A.J. has partial custody of his son, who lives with us part of the week and some weekends," Maddie told us. "A.J. can't move because it's in his agreement that he stay in the neighborhood where his son's mother lives. So we moved into his place, but my daughter's school is twenty minutes away. On days when A.J.'s son stays with us, I pick him up at the bus stop after school and then drive and pick up my daughter."

Logistics like these initially seem a bit daunting, but you'll work them out and they'll soon become the norm.

WHAT ABOUT CHANGES IN CHILD CUSTODY?

Although your husband's children currently may live with their mother, sometimes these situations change. The *Sturm und Drang* of adolescence can make kids decide they want to live with the other parent. Talk about how you'll cope if his children become part of your daily life.

"Kids, We Have Some Good News . . ."

How do we prepare our kids for the move? We want their transition to be as smooth as possible.

How you handle this with children will depend on their ages, whether they're still living at home and your relationship with them. One woman with young children moved in with her fiancé while he was still dealing with a lengthy divorce. She says if they had to do it again, they'd wait to move in together until after they were married. She says now it might have helped her children, who had struggled with divorce, to feel more secure with her new mate.

If combining your households means your children will need to change schools (and your custody agreement allows it), it might be an easier adjustment for the child if you move during summer vacation.

WHEN HE'S WIDOWED (AND HE HAS KIDS)

My boyfriend's a widower, and I've moved into his house. We're very happy together, but I feel like I'm living with a ghost. There are family photos everywhere; many of her clothes are still in the closet; he hasn't even moved the furniture around. How do I make changes without seeming insensitive toward him and his children?

This situation does require sensitivity, but the Garter Brides will help you make things easier and there's no need to rush.

Remember, if something were to happen to the man you love, you wouldn't just erase him from your life. He had a life before you, but things change. He's with you now and wants to be with you.

If his late wife's stuff is still around, whatever you do, don't throw it out. Even if he or his kids say it's OK, don't believe them. One woman we know moved in with a man whose wife had died several years earlier. She found his wife's things everywhere: address book, yearbooks, clothes, even her aprons still in the kitchen.

We don't have to tell you she made a big mistake by throwing them out. In spite of what they'd said, his kids did resent what she did.

Talk with your husband about how you'd like to handle this with his children. This is a very emotional issue, no matter how rational everyone seems about it. If you do anything the children misconstrue as disrespecting the memory of their mother, they'll never accept you. So if they give you permission to dispose of their mother's things, say, "I'm not comfortable doing that. When you're ready, you can come and pack them up." Set a time with them that is convenient for them to do it. It's a painful task for them, so if they don't keep to the schedule, just let it go.

Instead, ask your husband to help you pack up her things and carefully store them. Someday they'll be wanted, but even if not, his kids should know they can retrieve them whenever they wish.

continued

continued from last page

If there are family pictures around, naturally she'll be in them. They're part of your husband's history. Add a few photos of you and him, and of your family. Gradually the balance will shift to your new life. But there's plenty of time; you have the rest of your lives together.

A final word: when you, he and his kids are together, try not to refer to yourselves as a "family." Rather, say something like, "I'm so glad we can all be together to celebrate your dad's birthday." Calling yourselves a "family" should originate with the kids!

Who's Paying for What?

Below are some questions to ask when setting up housekeeping as a couple:

- What financial responsibilities will you each have for your home and related expenses?

- If one of you makes more money than the other, how will that affect your lifestyle and decisions about expenses?

- How do you both feel about financial changes? For example, if one of you owns a small business, how will you handle up and down years?

- Are you both OK with covering expenses if the other is out of work, and for how long?

- How much debt are you comfortable with? How will you pay off any existing debt?

- How do you each approach saving, spending and investing? If there are differences, how will you work those out? (If your finances are separate, you may feel whatever the other does with their own money is fine, but when you live together, your futures are commingled even if your finances aren't. How will you feel, for example, if he has money for a new car, but says "we" can't afford to fix the roof?)

Making Time for the Two of You

We work hard and so do our husbands, but we're careful that the pace doesn't creep up on our couple time, until our only exchanges involve stealing the blankets! "I have a girlfriend whose husband was staying at the office nightly until ten o'clock," one bride told us. "As a single man, he'd gotten into the habit of working overtime to fill a lot of lonely hours."

Some people have jobs defined by long or erratic hours, and even their down time can be interrupted by emergencies or other duties. How will you feel about having your guy work over vacation, leave social events early or not attend them? Would you go alone? Have a heart-to-heart. Here again, your maturity will help. "We didn't struggle over whose career needs came first," Tyra says. "He accepted my long work hours. I love him for that."

Everyone has busy periods; just make sure your relationship stays front and center.

KEEPING THINGS IN PERSPECTIVE

"Mark and I are both Type A personalities," Pat says. "Being in love put lots of things into a different perspective for both of us. Our priority is being together."

continued

continued from last page

Tish agrees. "It's easy to lose sight of the fact that the love you have for each other is the reason the two of you have this family in the first place. I read a bumper sticker that said, 'What have you done for your marriage today?' Good question! We try to do one thing, even if it's a small thing, that's about us every day."

Blending Beliefs

Many of the Garter Brides have married men who celebrate different religions than they do, and they've discovered many wonderful traditions (to say nothing of fabulous food) they never knew before.

If you have differences in religious practice, will you want each other to participate in services? Will you celebrate religious events and holidays in your home (including the cooking of traditional foods or family recipes), or will both of you go to be with other members of your family? These are things to consider.

"Where Should We Live?"

It's exciting to start out fresh in a new place, but often couples move into one person's home because of finances, space or proximity to work, children or school. In such cases, it means moving over (literally) to make space for the new roomie! Here are some perspectives on this from Garter Brides:

- "Buying and furnishing my own home was a victory I was proud of, so when Grant asked about living together, I took some time to think about it. We had spent the most time at his home, so it was a natural transition to move there. Moving some of my furniture in helped me with the change. Although I sometimes still feel nostalgic about my previous home because it represented an enormous accomplishment, I'm happy about my new life."

- "I love light and knew Casey's dark apartment wouldn't work for me. But it made logical sense at the time to live there, so I told myself, *Things will unfold*. After a few months I suggested, 'Let's look for a new place,' and he agreed. Eventually we found a place filled with sun and knew it was right for us."

- "I work at home and see clients very early in the morning. Aaron gave up living in a much larger house so my morning patterns and work life could stay the same. It made the transition easier for me."

- "Mike moved into my 700-square-foot affordable apartment with two huge dogs. I had two Jack Russell terriers! I nearly went nuts with the small space and all the animals, but it was worth it. We saved for two years and were able to buy the home we wanted."

Going the (Long) Distance

We live in different cities. How do we decide who moves?

The Garter Brides have pretty much covered the gamut of scenarios for making these kinds of decisions—especially Pat. Let's hear from her on this:

"Mark and I had been commuting between Atlanta and New York for over a year. Mark suggested that I move in with him in Atlanta. Moving away from his son was out of the question for both of us. Uprooting my life in New York would have meant changing jobs and leaving family and friends. I would be dependent on Mark for my social life, which just isn't the type of woman I am.

"So I took a deep breath . . . and said no: 'No ring, no wedding, no move!' It was just too much to ask of me without a real commitment to our relationship.

"Several months later, Mark proposed! Also, his son moved to another state. These changes opened up new possibilities for us. So we began peeling the decision onion.

"First, we decided that it made sense for Mark to move to New York. He could transfer to the New York office of his firm and I wouldn't have to pull up professional roots.

"Next, I preferred living in the city and Mark preferred the suburbs. We picked an affordable town that was an easy commute to the city for me and close to area airports for him. I finally have the small garden I've always wanted!

"It was thrilling to make these plans and put them in place. We were over the moon about being able to come home to each other. But it wasn't always easy living in the suburbs as a newlywed with Mark away so much. For over five years, I spent many Saturday nights at a local Italian restaurant with a book to keep me company. I also used the time to do more 'chick things,' which turned out to be a great way to transition my girlfriends and me into my new life. When Mark was home, we made sure it was extra special and romantic.

"When I look back on it now, it seems like a blip on the radar screen. It was crucial for us to work through these changes as a couple—it helped make us the good team that we are. In the end, it feels right."

Decisions you make about moving are great opportunities to practice how you'll approach decisions as a couple. "Alec and I had found a house in New Jersey that worked just fine for our two very different East Coast work commutes," Naomi told us. "But soon I could see that Alec wasn't happy. Often on weekends, while I stayed home with my young son, he would visit his teenage daughter in Chicago. He really missed being with her every day and found that staying in a hotel just didn't foster the easy hang-out time he wanted with her, so he decided that he should get a little apartment out there. I feared our marriage

QUESTIONS TO ASK BEFORE YOU RELOCATE

Before you move, ask yourself some important questions, including:

- If I move, will my career stay at the same level? If not, will it get there within six months to a year?

- Will I like the way I'm living as much or more than the way I'm living now?

- Will my commute be better or worse?

- How will I feel if I miss all my friends?

- Do I have any friends in the area, and if not, are there some interesting ways to make new ones?

- Do I like the location as much as I like the guy?

- What activities do I like doing alone? Can I do them if I move?

wouldn't get a strong start if he had another place to call home. Also, it would send the wrong message to his daughter—she needed to know that her dad had made a strong commitment to our life together back in New Jersey, and that nothing about it was temporary.

"When I explained how I felt about it to Alec, he understood the mixed messages he'd risked sending to both his daughter and to me. Instead, he made sure she spent more school vacation time with us. Now, several years later, she's actually come to live with us, and we're all really pleased about it."

One way to give a new location a trial run: sublet or lease your home and rent for a year. Then you can change the plan if an area that seemed appealing on a short visit turns out not to be the best choice for day-to-day life.

Last but not least, if you have no contacts in your new town, call all your Garter Bride pals and start a network for making new friends. They may be able to fix you up on a "friend blind date"! Then turn to your sweetheart and toast your flexibility as you embark on this new adventure side by side.

Married Across the Miles

Some couples maintain long-distance marriages, often because of job responsibilities—and sometimes because they find creative ways for two to enjoy the ideal lifestyle previously relished by one! While a younger couple's families might frown on this, for mature couples it can be a happy solution when two full and satisfying lives are joined. Long-distance marriages can succeed, although they're not for everyone. Much depends on the unique blend of your personalities, work and financial circumstances and geographic/lifestyle situation.

Needs a Little Work?

We've found a place that needs fixing up—actually, it could use a whole new kitchen! Should we share expenses for repairs and other big costs?

There's nothing like home repair or decorating to, uh, fortify your bond with your man. As one bride notes: "My husband says every engaged couple should clean out closets and wallpaper a bathroom together before getting married!" Read on for our advice—which can apply to any improvements you undertake in your love nest.

- ■ *Make sure you're each comfortable with what it costs.* Before participating in any major improvements, ask yourself: *If the relationship ends, would I be OK with the financial arrangement we made?*

■ *Split purchases, not costs.* A friend of ours moved with her boyfriend into his newly purchased home. He was renovating his kitchen and they split the cost of the appliances. She thought it was going to be happily ever after. Alas, they broke up. She wanted her money back. He refused. If they'd split purchases, not costs—if she'd bought the washer and he the dryer—at least she'd have come away with something. Lesson: split costs evenly if you can, and by item. That way no one has to take a hacksaw to the couch!

■ *If there's stuff you can't do on your own and you have to hire outside help, only one of you should deal with them.* When Ann and Irv had to have their kitchen rewired for a new fuse box, they decided that since Ann's schedule was a little more flexible, she should be the one to check on how things were going. That way, she and Irv could be "good cop, bad cop." "It made the experience relatively easy on all three of us: Irv, me and the electrician."

Building the Home Team

He doesn't like my couch. I don't like his collection of college softball trophies. He doesn't understand why I have "all those shoes and shampoos." I don't understand why his socks live wherever he drops them. Pretty much everything about our styles clash—but we love each other! How can we reconcile our differences?

When two adults move in together, sometimes that "invaded space" feeling is unavoidable. How do we know about that, you ask?

Pat: "I came with six sets of dishes and twenty-seven cake plates."

Ann: "We never lived together before; we had to learn how to divide up the responsibilities."

Tish: "I'm pretty messy and John's really neat. Once he politely asked me if I'd throw away the envelopes when I opened the mail. To this day I remember looking right at him and asking, 'What envelopes?'"

One bride laughed. "The moving-in advice I got included things like, 'Don't go to bed angry' and 'Make sure you have a date night every week.' I wish they'd said, 'Try to use separate bathrooms!'"

Here are some brides' ideas for making it work:

- **Have a let's-get-real conversation about housekeeping.** It might go something like this: "Let's not make promises we can't keep. Let's figure out what we'll do about housework, yard work, laundry and all that. If there's something one of us just won't do, let's make a plan to deal with it. If we cook less and order takeout more, can we afford it? How often will laundry get done?"

- **Set some ground rules, and take your time.** Ann recalls, "We decided to bring to our new apartment only things we both liked. That eliminated a lot and led to a lot of collaboration, because our tastes were quite different. We took our time putting our home together and it was really worth it—we both love how our place looks."

ENTERTAINING IDEAS

It's fun to imagine how you'll socialize as a couple. How do you both feel about entertaining and going out? Which would you rather host: an impromptu potluck or a dinner party with your best dishes? What about toasting at a New Year's bash versus curling up with a good movie till you kiss at midnight? Social style isn't generally a deal breaker, but radically different expectations should be discussed.

■ *Trust that two heads are better than one.* Is your guy a sports nut, watching every game known to mankind? Or a stock market follower, soaking up financial news 24/7? This is where being a little older helps: you don't need to tiptoe around. Ask for things you need to help you to live peacefully and happily together. If your spouse is a TV junkie, you may have to negotiate silence. Here are some possible solutions: have things your respective ways on alternating days, set a lower volume level, agree on a time limit or on specific must-see programs, put a small TV or radio in another room and close the door, wear headphones. Put your heads together and know that you will find a way.

■ *Set boundaries—literally.* Says one bride: "My husband is a 'collector,' whereas I clean house all the time. He works at home, and it's OK if he keeps his junk in his work area, but occasionally it spills into the bedroom, and we have a heart-to-heart. I say, 'Honey, do you realize you've got twelve books on your nightstand and about six weeks' worth of daily newspapers?' 'I do?' he says with wide-eyed amazement. I know that if I were in my twenties I would be ranting and raving constantly. Now, though it does drive me nuts on occasion, I'm realistic about the situation and realize that's part of the package."

■ *Suggestions work better than orders.* "I wouldn't like it if my husband gave me orders, so I try not to do it with him. My mother told me something wise. She said people like to feel that things are their idea. I've learned it works much better to suggest something than say, 'We have to do this.'"

■ *Make it a puzzle, not a problem.* "My husband loves team sports and strategy, so I pose a problem as a team strategy puzzle: 'How do you think we can solve this?' Often his solution is better than mine, and he wants to be in charge of executing it—which means I don't have to!"

- **Love, like work, can be wonderful without being perfect.** We don't expect to love every aspect of our jobs. That balanced view applies to relationships, too. If one of you feels you're coming out on the short end of the stick too often, that can and should be addressed, just like on the job. "I don't expect things to be perfect, as I did in my twenties," one bride observed. "Now I expect us to work on it."

- **Live and learn.** Jaclyn says, "I taught him to do laundry (if you can imagine living for forty years without knowing how!) and now he helps with it. Just last night, I instituted our first laundry folding party in the bedroom while we watched television. It's a new family tradition!"

- **Change is good, when you both change for love.** Vanessa notes the challenges and changes of moving in with Stewart: "He was forced to become more Type A; I was forced to become less Type A. He had to move across the country and learn how to make vinaigrette, put his underwear in the hamper and operate a vacuum cleaner; after living on my own for a while (and liking it just fine), I had to learn how to make room for another person—and put up with toenail clippings on the carpet, channel surfing and other bachelor behavior."

- **Adopt the "five things" rule.** Leslie told us, "My advice to mature brides is: Name five things that are absolutely essential to you. Ask for what you need and be flexible about the rest. The relationship is more important than a sofa."

Your Stuff . . . My Stuff . . . Our Stuff

"We still have three very large soccer trophies waiting to find the right place. We also have various things I don't think belong in a house, such as a truck bumper. I have to remember that he's had to make the *big* adjustment of not having a garage and space for his tools, and he's parted with many things from his past. We may buy a new house in the future, but we've agreed to stay put for at least a year."

FROM ANNOYING TO ENDEARING

Here are some things Garter Brides (and their grooms) learned to live with and even love:

- Tish smiles when she remembers that John always says he has one square foot in the house that's all his: the chair where he puts his briefcase. "He knows our house is always going to be pretty cluttered, but he's really good about it."

- One bride says, "Jack is very particular about the laundry, so he handles that completely. We grocery-shop together most of the time, and share the cooking and cleaning up. Heavy housework is more of an issue. In the beginning I did the lion's share, and I resented it. When I got a job with a longer commute, he started helping out more and realized how much I'd been doing, and he really pitched in."

- "I have a terrible habit of wandering into my husband's office and chatting away when he's in the middle of something or when he's reading the newspaper, which is very important in his daily routine. He'd never close his door to me, so in return I try not to go bouncing in there all the time. I work on saving our chats for mealtimes. Being a chatterbox, I find this requires real willpower!"

- "Garth was so helpless in the kitchen that I actually thought he might be faking it: he'd look in the fridge and be unable to find a thing! I've taught him how to heat up leftovers, and he can make his own breakfast. He's an appreciative eater and loves what I cook. But *I* cook."

continued

continued from last page

- "I do almost all the dishwashing, usually at night before bed because I hate facing a sinkful of dishes the next morning. So who could blame me for moving through the job pretty fast, usually after I take out my contact lenses, right before I hit the sack? Which means that sometimes there's a little food left on a few items. Once my husband took a knife out of the drainer and held it up so I could see one side still completely covered with peanut butter. And he said with a tolerant smile: 'The legend continues.'"

"My husband is a herpetologist—a reptile specialist. We have an alligator and multiple snakes. No, this is not my thing, but it's part of the package."

"My guy brought very little with him except his grandmother's rocking chair and some old family favorites, but he does want his things around, and at first I didn't realize how important that was to him. I have to be careful not to be inadvertently controlling."

Tish remembers, "John brought along a stuffed bird in a glass dome that had been his grandmother's. There was some family story about how it talked and was her most prized possession. I thought it was kind of creepy, but the kids think it's funny. I have a feeling that wherever we live, that bird's coming with us!"

"We made a project about finding just the right items for our place and spent many happy Saturdays browsing in thrift shops. One day we found a couch in bad shape 'for sale as is.' Every couch we'd seen was heavy and overstuffed. We instantly knew this one was the right style. It was the first thing we bought and fixed up together. Every time I look at it, I remember that wonderful day."

"I Love You Just the Way You Are . . . Really"

You've been together long enough to know each other well. But part of the fun of moving in together is that there are some things you don't discover about each other's personalities until you move in. And some insights come to light over time, as you live and grow together.

This is where your fellow Garter Brides can really help you by offering their experiences and wisdom. Our best discovery: all of us have found that we can change, and so can our husbands.

"There are things about me that I thought were etched in stone," Pat says, "but Mark and I have opened new worlds to each other both in our interests and in the way we see things. I appreciate and love that."

Tish adds, "John cares about small things that honestly never even entered my mind before we met, but they do now because they matter to him. For instance, he always fills the car with gas when the tank is a quarter full so the kids and I will never run out of gas. Before we met, I'd have driven for miles without filling up, but this is one of his ways of showing us he cares, so now I try to do it, too."

"My husband is a lot more energetic than I used to be—I was a slug!" Susan says. "But he energized me. Now we get out and do things, and my mother looks at me and says, 'Where did this come from?' I know where it came from, and so does my husband. That's good for both of us."

"A couple in love gives each other growth spurts," Ann observes. "Your strengths complement each other, but you also push each other to grow in a positive way. I love having that constant exposure to another point of view on life."

Tomato, Tomahto . . . Whatever!

"You're impetuous!" he says. "You can't make up your mind!" she says. Can this marriage be saved? Actually, it's thriving—Ann and Irv have been ecstatically wedded for seventeen years!

We find the differences between us and our husbands make us stronger together than we were alone—and we were pretty impressive alone! But just because we complement each other doesn't mean we don't sometimes hit speed bumps when solving problems or making decisions as a couple. "Irv's always telling me I'm very effective and accomplished," Ann says. "But when it comes to joint decisions, although he appreciates my skills and may eventually accept my choice, he still finds it necessary to 'ponder.' I've learned not to try to talk him into things."

You may have different social styles, too. "I love Irv's zest for life. He has lots of friends and wants to share everything with me. It's a great compliment, but a little exhausting. I connect well with people but find large groups draining. One good strategy: we plan ahead to leave a party for dinner with another couple. It extends the socializing, which Irv likes, but on a more intimate scale, which I like."

Here are some additional insights from other Garter Brides:

- "The moment my husband comes home, he likes to turn on the TV, the radio, et cetera. I need to have some silence. We had to consciously agree on some time for peace and quiet."
- "It was a big change for him to be with someone so independent."
- "He's much more romantic than I am. He says things like, 'I want to take you skiing in Aspen,' even though we both know we can't afford that until we pay off our wedding and honeymoon. But I've learned to let him be the romantic he is. He said to me once, 'You wouldn't like me if I weren't this way,' and he's right."
- "We're always at our best when we're operating as a team. If we hit a snag, we remind each other that we're in it together. It's a wonderful

feeling to know that we're both looking in the same direction and taking care of each other."

If you start to wonder whether you married a (really attractive) Martian, call a trusted girlfriend and vent, laugh and regain your perspective. With our fellow Garter Brides as our sounding boards, we find we come back refreshed, resourceful and better able to bridge our differences—including how we solve problems.

NESTING NOTES

"When I was younger, I wanted things done my way! Now I realize arguing only has a negative impact. If you really feel strongly about something and it will cause an argument, take a break from the situation until you can come back and talk about it and work it out. Don't hold onto anger. Remember that neither of you is completely right."

From Books to Bungee Jumping: Activities Alone and Together

Whether it's best-friends brunch, book club, pizza with the guys, poker night, pottery class, season hockey tickets, the ballet or weekend softball, we all have things we love to do. When your hobbies don't quite match up, how do you each feel about doing some things on your own? It's something that both of you should talk about.

"My husband had a lifelong Sunday tennis game with his best friend, his father and his father's best friend," Chrissie said. "He was gone most of the day, not getting home till late Sunday afternoon. I accepted it for a long time, but after our baby was born, I felt a change was needed. I was working and taking care of the baby, and I fell into the habit of doing the housework when he was playing on Sunday. It wasn't easy for him to give up this tradition, but we talked about it in terms of the new responsibilities we now had as a family, and he understood." (An alternative solution from Ann's ever-thoughtful Irv, who also loves a good tennis game: they could have played monthly, not weekly.)

Other Garter Brides told us how they make different interests work:

- "Our tastes in music are very, very different, and that's an issue. Part of it is that he's seven years younger than I am. I tolerate his music and have introduced him to jazz, which he now has an ear for. I also hate commercial radio, particularly in the car, and he has now developed an interest in noncommercial programming. It's something we keep working on together."

- "Although Mark and I have developed many common interests, we don't have standoffs about interests we don't share. If I want to do something that he's not crazy about, it's an opportunity for me to get together with a friend. Truth is, as independent as I am, I always prefer being with him."

- "I did what I call 'adopt-a-hobby.' My husband's a NASCAR buff. At first I watched the races on TV just to keep him company. But when I started paying attention and asking him questions, I found I appreciated the technical demands of the sport. Now I attend the Daytona 500—and love it. No one's more surprised about this than I am!"

- "We pursue separate interests, but we both come up with things to do together so we keep building experiences as a couple. It doesn't have to be expensive or a big deal. The other day I e-mailed Bill at work: 'Friday night the museum is open late. Let's go see that new photography exhibit.'"

Maybe there's an activity you can take up together? It could be bowling, Frisbee, swing dancing, golf, running, camping, kayaking, drawing, photography, political work, volunteering or something else you've always wanted to try! One Garter Bride couple gave each other snowshoes for Christmas. They love exploring the winter wonderland around their home.

THEN VS. NOW

"At twenty I'd have turned myself inside out to learn how to ski if it were my boyfriend's passion. I tried it once with Irv and hated the lines, the lifts, the layers of clothes. Now I walk around the town and meet him for dinner. We both have lots of things to share from the day."

Tish adds, "John loves to go fishing but I admit the open sea scares me unless it is dead calm. So over the years we've decided it makes more sense for me to wait for him to get home and we'll cook the fish he caught together. (*If* he catches a fish!)"

"Mark is a car nut. Me, if it has an FM radio, I'm happy. Sometimes for his birthday I get him a gift certificate to a driving school where he can drive race cars with a passenger—not me, but his son. It's a win-win. I don't have to smell the fumes and clutch the armrests. He gets to drive cool cars and spend time with his son. And he adores me for giving him 'the best present ever'!"

Speaking of hobbies and time off, what's your idea of a great vacation? Ann tells a funny crossed-wires story about this: "The first time Irv and I went away together for longer than a weekend, we rented a place at the beach. I'd brought out some special recipes I wanted to make, but he kept insisting we go out for dinner. One day I burst into tears. 'You don't want me to cook for you,' I sobbed. He was dismayed. He thought that since it was my vacation and I worked hard, he didn't want me to have to bother with cooking! He totally misread me and I misread him. We straightened it out and that night when I did cook (bay scallops, pasta with spinach and ricotta, and

I can't remember what else), he said, 'You're terrific. What a lucky guy I am!' We laugh about it now, but it was an interesting lesson in how often we make assumptions that a simple conversation could set right."

WORK CAN BE PLAY, TOO!

"Introduce each other to your worlds and your work," Ann says. "As a producer, I attended an annual weekend event showcasing theatrical work in development, with four or five shows a day you might not see anywhere else. Irv knew I adored it. One year I asked him to go with me. He saw a new side of me through seeing the kind of work I loved. We both had a wonderful time."

Don't Worry About Everything . . . Just the Important Things

When you and your partner combine personal honesty with an appreciation of who you are, you create a climate of mutual respect where love can flourish. Andrea says, "My husband never went to college; I have a Ph.D. He likes motorcycles; I'm not a fan. And his talents aren't in written or spoken language; mine are. But he is very intuitive about people; he is wise; he can make something from nothing; he is very creative; he has good, long-term friends; he can fix anything; he has a heart of gold and would help anyone; he is affectionate and kind. And when he smiles, you can see right down into his beautiful soul."

* * *

We know that a terrific life between two loving people is waiting for you. One Garter Bride says, "I know when we're together we're going to laugh. We love being together, even though we managed perfectly well on our own."

Pat says, "Whenever my husband and I walk in the door after a trip, I always take a deep breath and say, 'It's good to be home.' And he always looks at me and says, 'You're my home.'"

When Ann wished Irv a happy birthday, he said, "Every day's my birthday when I'm with you."

That is our wish for you.

GROOVY MOVIES: MISMATCHED!

Odd couples and couples at odds has been a goldmine for Hollywood. For us that means countless hours of entertainment. So turn your back on the dirty dishes and cuddle up to watch one of these films.

Adam's Rib	*Mostly Martha*
It Happened One Night	*The Odd Couple*
Last Chance Harry	*Pride and Prejudice*
When Harry Met Sally	

CHAPTER 6
Dollars and Common Sense
Grown-up Issues for Grown-up Brides

Your life has changed and you're overjoyed! You've found the man of your dreams and you're in love. You trust him with your heart, but how about your wallet, no matter how full or empty it may be? There's a lot more of everything in your life now: family, property, bank accounts and financial obligations—not to mention goals and aspirations. Both of you have worked for years to get what you have, and now you're beginning a new phase of your lives when you can plan your financial future together. But what exactly is the best way to do that?

There's no denying that money is a "hot button issue" with lots of emotions swirling around it: fear, safety, certainty and uncertainty, control, power and trust (to name a few). Often relationships with money start in your childhood, and your parents' relationship with money may have had an effect on the feelings you have about it now as an adult.

As one bride told us, "From the day I was six and my father handed me a plastic bank shaped like a pirate's chest, complete with a lock, I have never been able to feel comfortable with money. I have made money, invested it, spent it and given it away, but it *still* makes me nervous."

In your twenties you're just starting out and building your life, but now as an older bride you and your husband may be at the height of your earning years or planning what you want to do for retirement. You're partners and now have a wonderful opportunity to deal with whatever financial challenges you may face as a team.

As Tish says, "By the time we were in our mid-thirties, most of us had been through various kinds of financial situations and learned from them. Experience is a huge plus when you're a grown-up. You both have insight you can use to help you make new and better decisions."

Those Kitchen Table Talks

"Dollars and common sense" conversations about finances and related topics such as retirement, wills and life insurance aren't exactly romantic. But they're absolutely necessary before you both start making "plans." They are truly some of the "big" relationship topics, along with children, religion and where to live.

When the two of you sit down to discuss these things, you may find that as adults who built your own lives before you got together, you're combining multiple, and sometimes very different, interests and it may take some time to get on the same page. But as a grown woman, you're accustomed to figuring things out. The good news is, now there are two grown-ups in the room, so you can work things out together.

Although we're not financial professionals, in this chapter we'll highlight key issues for you to be aware of to spark ideas, questions and topics to discuss with your partner as you plan your financial future. Many of these have come up in our own lives or in the lives of the Garter Brides we interviewed. Our experiences vary widely: some of us married men who had more money than we did; some of us brought the booty (in every sense of the word!) and our men brought...

alimony and child support. Many couples confronted debt and some even bankruptcy. Many of us had to reconcile financial styles: who's a saver and who's a spender, who pays the bills as soon as they arrive and who doesn't, who keeps accounts separate and who combines them, even who wants to retire when. These issues arise with younger couples, too, but the stakes are higher when you're older because, as we've said, there's more of everything at stake.

So find a time to sit down to discuss your hopes, your fears and your goals about how to handle your money. It's important to decide what you want to accomplish together and when. Are one or both of you trying to get out of debt? Do you need to save for college for your kids, his kids or the kids you may have together? Are you supporting relatives? Do either of you owe alimony or child support payments, and if so, for how long?

GARTER BRIDE TIP

KEEP COOL

When you have these conversations, try to remain calm and not get too emotional. We also recommend that you don't try to discuss *everything* at once; just discuss a few things at a time.

Some people come to marriage with debts—from credit card debt to college loans and everything in between. But as common as debt is, it's hard to talk about. "I was having terrible financial problems when we married. It was very difficult for me to share this with Luis," Angie said.

When Danielle and her husband got married, both of them had credit card debt. They sat down together and made a plan on how they would get rid of the debt and buy a home. They made a budget and stuck to it. They created milestones—paying each card off one by one—and celebrated each victory. In five years, they were debt free and were able to buy a small home. Danielle told us that the key to their success was remembering that they were a team. This was a challenge they were facing together, and it worked.

If either or both of you are in debt from overspending, you have a win-win opportunity here: by helping your spouse spend wisely, you'll be helping yourself. A good first step is to figure out what motivates the spending. "Kurt is someone who doesn't hold back on things," Cara told us. "He's a hearty eater and a hearty spender. I think maybe this was how he showed love to himself. I had some credit card debt when we got engaged, but he had a lot of it. We're still in the process of getting through it. We need to make out a budget, but for now we're working on paying cash for things and using credit cards less. Also, he used to order stuff constantly from online catalogues, especially if it was 'on sale.' Then he'd get e-mail solicitations from all these places. We decided to use a different e-mail address for his online ordering, so the tempting solicitations wouldn't come to his personal e-mail. Little things like that help."

Sometimes having to think about someone else helps us set limits we might not set for ourselves. "Now he's aware that, for both our sakes, he needs to pay down that debt, and he's not resisting it," Cara said.

Remember, too, that some financial obligations do come to an end at some point. (This came as a surprise to some brides!) You may look ahead and think, *We have five more years of paying for this?* One bride remembers, "When we got married, Jerry's kids were five and seven and he was responsible for paying child support until they were twenty-one. I remember thinking that felt like forever, but the years slid past and one day it was behind us."

In any marriage there will be financial ups and downs. No jobs are cradle-to-grave anymore, and things change—that's part of life. But if you work to establish yourself as a team right from the get-go, you will be ready to handle these changes together.

Filling in the Financial Blanks

An important thing to remember when you get married as a mature bride is that the man in your life is also a grown-up who may have weathered financial storms at some point or been married before. It would be easy to think, *That's all in the past,* but you need to know what has happened before in his life and he needs to know what has happened in yours.

My husband and I have both been married before. He has children but I don't. Should we read each other's divorce agreements?

The Garter Brides' answer to this one: yes!

Talking about divorce, alimony and child support can be awkward, and you may not look forward to reading about the details of his divorce any more than he wants to read about yours, but it's super-important. Here are some key reasons why:

- *The marriages may be past tense, but the divorce agreements aren't.* These legal documents directly affect your life now and in the future, influencing decisions you will make as a couple about your income, employment, investments, retirement and possibly even where you will live. You need to know how much of your spouse's income will be going to support his ex-wife and/or his children, and for how long. One bride told us, "I didn't know until years after I got married that my husband's ex-wife was due a life insurance policy if he died. I had no idea this policy even existed. My girlfriends urged me to read his divorce agreement, but I honestly didn't think it was any of my business. Now I'm glad I did."

Another bride, whose new husband still had years of alimony to pay, learned that if he died owing alimony, the first monies of his life insurance policy would go to pay off the alimony, with the remainder coming to her. These are just two examples of the kind of information that must be shared so the two of you can make reasonable decisions about your future.

- **Maintenance and alimony affect a joint tax return.** Alimony/maintenance payments are tax deductible. If you're signing and filing a joint tax return with your spouse, you should know what that deduction is.

- **If children are involved, you must know what support they're entitled to.** Children need to be protected by all the adults involved in their lives. In fact, one way to broach the subject of sharing your divorce agreements might be, "We need to read these documents to make sure we understand all the obligations to the children."

We suggest you read the actual documents, not rely on memory when discussing them. The stress of divorce and the passage of time can create memory gaps. Also, in the heat of the moment, we don't always make wise choices in divorce agreements, and a new spouse should be clued into the issues. Belinda told us, "I made a big mistake racing through my divorce agreement without taking the time to get advice on what I should be doing. I had an attorney, but I wish I'd had someone wise about money read my divorce agreement before I signed it. Eric thinks my settlement was a financial disaster. I just wanted it over with and would have signed anything to get custody of my daughter."

What's Up with a Prenup?

I've been married before and have a son, but my husband has never been married and doesn't have any kids. Do we need a prenup?

Some of the Garter Brides have had prenups (prenuptial agreements) and some have not, but there are some important things to remember here. Deciding to get a prenup does not mean you're thinking that the two of you will get divorced. If having a document like this makes either of you feel more safe and secure, then you should definitely get one.

Remember, you've been taking care of yourself for years and are now moving on to the next stage in your life. You're a smart woman who has managed finances on your own, and you don't want to be blindsided by something coming from left field. Knowledge is power.

Writing a prenup can also be a remarkably bonding experience in the most mature kind of way, because it's a major step you're taking together about a very serious subject that affects you and those you love.

One bride refused to marry her husband without a prenup. She had been financially wiped out by her divorce and even had to shoulder some of her ex-husband's debts. So even though the new man in her life didn't think they needed one, because, unlike her, he had never been married or had children, he went along with it because it meant so much to her.

How does it work? Basically, you'll each produce a personal financial statement that shows each of your assets and debts. If it turns out later that some information from either of you was not shared, the prenup will be invalidated.

WHEN TO DRAW UP A PRENUP

Draw up your prenup as soon as possible after getting engaged.

Here are six grown-up reasons for writing a prenup:

1. *To protect your hard-earned assets.* "I've always been a very independent working woman. When I got married he wanted a prenup, and I realized I needed one, too. I didn't have children, but I wanted to help my niece and nephew with their college tuition if I could."

2. *To protect a business.* "Colin hated asking me to sign a prenup, but because he owned his own business and had been devastated financially when his previous marriage ended, I understood why it was so important to him." The same protection, of course, could be applied to a female business owner. We know a woman whose business was supporting her and her husband. When they divorced, he got the house and she paid him alimony for three years so she could keep all her business profits and retirement income.

3. *As security against unexpected events.* "One thing about being a mature bride is that you know the unexpected happens more often than not. It isn't that I thought we'd get divorced, but you never know if an ex-spouse or a lawsuit might jeopardize your financial stability. We both came to our marriage with assets we'd worked hard for and wanted to protect. In my twenties, pretty much all I brought to my marriage was my toothbrush. In my fifties, I had

things I'd worked hard for. I didn't want all of that to disappear if, for example, my husband got sued in his business."

4. *For financial and emotional stability.* Corinne says, "When I got divorced, I had the rug pulled out from under me. My son was six months old and nothing was in my name. When I remarried, *not* having a prenup was a deal breaker for me. I never wanted to feel that vulnerable again. Ironically, my new husband was a tax attorney, but he was more romantic, and I was the one insisting on the prenup!"

5. *To protect and reassure children.* A prenup can give peace of mind to grown children, and it's never too late to have one. One bride remarried at seventy-nine to a man a couple of years older than she. Both were widowed; she had four grown children and he had none. They had a prenup that ensured that all her assets would go to her children.

   When Janet got married for the second time, she wanted to make sure her children inherited the property she brought to the marriage. As she told us, "My husband and I both believe what's his is his and what's mine is mine, and we felt a prenup was very important."

6. *To keep state laws from controlling your finances.* Depending on where you live, divorce laws may decree equitable distribution: property acquired during the marriage may be split 50/50 regardless of who owns it. A prenup allows the two of you to decide how your property will be divided in such a situation, rather than having it dictated by the laws of your state. So, for example, if you own the house the two of you are living in, the prenup can stipulate that you keep the house in the event of divorce.

   Remember, if one of you moves to another state so the two of you can live together, you both will be subject to the marital and estate laws in the state of your joint residency. Since these laws differ from state to state, be sure to investigate how they may affect the terms of your prenup, will or other legal and financial issues before you decide to move.

NO WILLS? NO WAY!

My friend and her fiancé made out new wills before they got married. Do we really need to do this?

We know women who have had trouble facing writing wills. In fact, we have girlfriends whose wills still sit on their kitchen tables unsigned two years after they've been drafted. It's important to remember that a will reduces paperwork and anxiety for those left behind and clarifies how you wish to have your worldly goods distributed to those you care about. As Ann says, "A will is a gift you give your spouse. If something happens, you know what his wishes are and he knows yours."

One bride got married for the first time when she was twenty-three and became a widow when her husband died suddenly, leaving her with a young daughter. She didn't have a will when she remarried fifteen years later and her new husband moved into her house. He put a lot of time and money into renovating the house, but she regrets that they never discussed who would eventually inherit it. She feels it should go to her daughter, since it was bought by her father and was part of his estate. But with all the work her new husband has done fixing and maintaining it, she feels he has some stake in it, too. Now she doesn't know what to do.

Here's one solution that has worked for other Garter Brides: leave the house to your children while leaving your husband money or other assets comparable to his investment. Still, it's awkward to resolve issues like this after the fact—it's much better to discuss these matters up front as part of your dollars-and-common-sense conversations before you get married.

Andie uses her parents as an example of another solution: "My mother and stepfather set up their wills so my stepdad could stay in their house (which had been my mother's) for life. When he died, the house would pass to my sister and me. If he chose to make improvements, he understood the house would still go to us and his assets would go to his kids."

GARTER BRIDE TIP

A DIFFERENT WAY TO THINK ABOUT WILLS

Planning for the future is one more way of taking care of each other. If you think about writing a will as something you're doing for the people you love, it may make it easier to put it on the to-do list.

Another important reason to have a will is so you don't put your spouse, kids and stepkids in the position of hashing out who gets what. "I've known my stepchildren since they were in grade school. They're grown now and we get along great," Holly told us. "But I know my husband is the unifying element between us. If he dies, we'll all need to make more of an effort to stay connected. The last thing we'd need is to fight over money."

We also advise brides to review their wills every few years. It's easy to forget, but it's important to see if any updates are needed. Life changes over time, and you may discover your will should, too. Ask yourself these questions:

- **Has your family changed?** If you have a child, you need to name a guardian. Zoe said, "I appointed my brother guardian of my kids but made sure it was his decision as to whether he would raise them. I didn't want him to feel pressured to raise two young kids." Valerie told us, "I decided I wanted my kids to live with a friend's family until they completed high school, so they wouldn't have to change schools." You may have had a grandchild since you wrote your will. These are the sorts of things you don't usually think about when marrying at twenty-one but are natural and necessary when you get married as a grown-up.

- **Has your professional life changed?** Kyra said, "When we first wrote our wills, I was in beauty school and now I have my own salon. I needed to add information in my will about who would inherit the business."

- **Did I overlook something?** Because blended families are complex, you might have overlooked an important issue: "Phil's daughter was named executor of both of our estates," Francesca told us, "which at first seemed like the simplest way to set things up, but I recently realized that since I'm not her mother, she shouldn't have to be responsible for me. My son is old enough now, so I've named him as my executor."

We also recommend that you get a living will and a health care proxy, and that you and your spouse have a power of attorney for each other that will allow you to make important decisions for each other should that become necessary. All of these documents are easily available online.

So here are our big questions:

- Do you have a will?

- Does your husband?

- If you do have one, now that you're married should it be changed?

- If you don't have one, what is keeping you from writing it?

IT'S 10:00 P.M.—
DO YOU KNOW WHERE YOUR PAPERWORK IS?

- Prenup
- Health care proxy

- Will
- Power of attorney
- Insurance policies

- Living will
- Divorce agreements

All of these are important documents, and you want to know where to find them if you need them quickly. Some brides admit they're not totally sure where these documents are stored. We recommend that you check the Internet for websites that provide checklists to help you keep track of all your legal, personal and financial information and monthly expenses.

"Honey, Did You Pay the Electric Bill?"
"Um . . . What Electric Bill?"

You may discover that you and your husband have very different personal styles in dealing with money. Both of you will bring your past experiences to this subject. As Tish says, "I'd been single and handling my own money for so long that when John and I got together I couldn't quite imagine revealing everything about my financial situation to him. Then one day I realized we would soon be filing a joint tax return, so he was going to know all about it anyway. We laughed about our different bill-paying styles. He pays his bills in a neat stack, all at once. I pay them sort of here and there, when they come in. He uses a letter opener to open his bills; I rip the envelopes to shreds."

GARTER BRIDE TIP

IT'S IN THE FILE?

If the man in your life says, "I have them all in a file," make sure you know where the file *is*! As Ann says, "Irv told me where everything is, but I said to him, 'If anything happens to you I'll be devastated and certainly not able to remember all of this. Please put it in writing for me.' And he did. I never look at it, but I know it's there."

Should my husband and I have one bank account or separate accounts?

Until you get a clear sense of each other's financial philosophies and day-to-day habits, you may find it sensible when newly married to keep separate accounts along with a joint checking account that you each contribute to and draw from for household expenses and things you buy together. Later, you can decide if that arrangement works for both of you or if you want to modify it.

Once we started asking other Garter Brides how they make their finances work, we found that there are as many creative solutions as there are couples! Here are a few of the things we heard to spark your ideas and conversations:

■ "We opened a joint checking account for household expenses and decided how much we'd each contribute monthly, reevaluating it every three months to see if we needed to add or decrease our contributions. Gary kept his checking account for child support payments, alimony and personal things. I kept mine for my personal things. It sounds like a lot of accounts for one household, but actually it was easier to sort and track expenses."

■ Shauna told us, "Patrick oversees most of the bill paying, which I agreed to because I could tell this was a big issue for him, maybe a hangover from some problems in his previous marriage. But it was also important to me as an independent woman not to lose touch with those skills of managing money."

■ "My husband would prefer to handle all the bills, but I've been on my own for years and wasn't comfortable turning my money over to someone else. We have a joint checking account, but I have my own account, too. He balances all the accounts on his computer, which satisfies his need to keep on top of things. It might be easier if he handled everything, but that wouldn't feel good to me, so I still pay the bills."

■ "There was no financial transition with us. I did not blend my savings with his. I have my own bank accounts and so does he. I pay my bills and he pays his. Our financial styles are completely different—I'm a saver and he's a spender. He pays all his bills at the beginning of the month; I pay them as they're due."

■ "I pay the bills. Ned keeps the records and handles all the tax stuff. All our money is combined. There's one pot and we both dip into it."

Bankruptcy: It Does Happen

Nora and Owen had been married for four years when he started a construction company with his brother-in-law, Ben. Ben kept the books and Owen had no idea that every year their company was sinking further and further into debt until it was too late. Owen was forced to declare personal bankruptcy when their kids were four and six and Nora wasn't working. "Owen ended up staying home with the kids and I went back to work. It wasn't easy, but we made it through."

Separate accounts may also protect you if one of you suffers a bankruptcy; in that case the other's assets will be protected. While there's no way to predict such an event, if the possibility of a bankruptcy is of concern to you, consider keeping at least some of your assets separate, especially those each of you brought into the marriage.

Life Changes: Guaranteed!

When you get married later in life, maturity and experience have already taught you that things change—then change again. Jobs come and go, children move out and sometimes back in, people fall ill and get better, aging parents get older. It's all part of life. What we hope doesn't change is your feelings for the man in your life and his feelings for you. Financial decisions are ongoing and ever-changing, but remember two heads are better than one when it comes to figuring out what's best to do.

Lucia went to work on a typical Friday and knew something was wrong. Sure enough, her boss called her into the office and told her their division had been closed and she had an hour to leave her office. It took her all weekend to find the perfect time to tell her husband but in the end she just burst out with it. When she did, he hugged her and told her, "We'll figure something out."

When Terri's daughter, who'd become a single mom at twenty, hit a rough patch, she asked Terri and her husband Marty to take care of four-year-old Haley. Terri didn't know what to do. Of course, she would take Haley in a heartbeat, but who would watch the child while she and Marty were at work, and how would they pay for it? She called Marty, and even before she could get out the whole story, he told her, "Go pick up Haley. We'll make it work." The happy ending was that their neighbor was delighted to watch Haley in exchange for Marty helping fix up her house.

Becoming a strong financial team will help you weather the inevitable ups and downs of life. Admitting how you feel and venting about your financial fears or letting him vent to you about his will help you both over the rough times.

You Want to Retire *When*?

Here again is one of the realities of getting married as a grown-up: couples who marry in their twenties can "grow" their retirement dreams together, while couples marrying later in life may have nurtured their separate retirement goals for years and now need to combine those visions.

Whether you're totally in sync or wildly divergent on the when and what of retirement, it's something to discuss and plan together—including the how.

Here are a few questions to get you started:

- How old would you like to be when you retire?
- What's your ideal lifestyle in retirement, including where you'd like to live and the kinds of things you'd like to do?
- What will be your sources of income?
- Do you have a goal amount in mind for retirement savings?
- Do you have a financial plan for reaching that goal?

THE POINT OF IT ALL

Remember the most important thing: now, as you plan for your retirement years, you can look forward to spending them with the man you love.

Being a grown-up in the real world is a complex process, and dealing with financial issues is just one part of it. But remember, things change over time. Problems that seem huge now will diminish, though there are bound to be some kind of challenges ahead. What's different is that now you have the support of the man in your life to bounce ideas off of, someone who can offer suggestions and be there for you no matter what happens.

CHAPTER 7
"You're Wearing *White?*"
Having Your Wedding, Your Way

He just proposed—and you said yes. You're both giddy with joy. When you share your news, some people may be surprised, most will be delighted—and some might think you've been married all along!

By now you know we're shamelessly romantic (and just plain shameless). Which explains why we encourage you, whether or not you're yet engaged, to shamelessly dream your wedding dreams. To help those dreams along, we'll share a wealth of wedding ideas from fellow grown-up brides, from the elegantly simple to the simply sumptuous. What will *you* choose for your celebration? Dinner and dancing by candlelight? A Buddhist-accented garden party? A picnic with guests in Bermuda shorts? A bash with gospel singers? Our brides have been there, done all that.

We'll also help you imagine who you'll be on that special day: perhaps a queen in white satin and Belgian lace, a goddess in a crystal-studded gown, a vintage vision in a 1920s frock, a cutie in a sundress, or a movie star in sleeveless, beaded gray chiffon (this bride let her hair match her dress, not bothering to cover the gray). Our brides looked and felt like these, and more.

We'll reveal how couples used their grown-up smarts to navigate common speed bumps on the way to the big day, keeping their spirits high and their love at the helm. Here's to the wedding of your dreams!

We're Engaged!

I'm engaged, and I'm thrilled, excited . . . and a little scared! I've wanted this for a long time—so why do I have the jitters?

You're not alone! As one bride wisely said, "When a man asks you to marry him when you're twenty, you say, 'Why not?' When a man asks you to marry him when you're forty, you ask, 'Why?'"

We wouldn't be writing this book if there weren't tons of fabulous reasons to be married—*and* if we didn't believe that grown-up women should always ask "Why?" when making important decisions about their lives.

Some of our brides quickly knew they'd found Mr. Right. One woman in her sixties met and got to know her future husband in a class they took together: "On the last day, he said, 'I'd hate to see us lose touch with each other. How about dinner sometime soon?' By the third or fourth such date, we found ourselves agreeing by the end of the meal that we'd get married. We knew each other's stories pretty well by then, and we both felt great comfort with each other."

More often, it took the brides we interviewed a bit of time to get to "I do." Sometimes there were logistical reasons: "Gene's divorce took five years, but within a day of getting the divorce he asked me to marry him."

No doubt about it, grown-up life can be complex. "Perry and I dated for seven years before marrying, and we didn't live together,"

Natasha told us. "When we met, he was forty-six and had two daughters just out of college; I was thirty and my daughters were seven and
five. The advice Perry got from friends and from his family counselor
was to take it slowly and make sure he wanted to raise two more children basically from the start. The advice I got from friends and family
was quite different. They were worried Perry might never commit to
marriage and I'd 'waste the best years of my life.' We both agreed living
together with two young children wasn't an option. When we finally
married, everyone was thrilled. His friends were convinced he was
making a good decision; my friends were happy I'd found someone
who took such good care of me and my girls and made me so happy."

Remember Tish and John, flying between cities on weekends?
Talk about a logistical nightmare! "As time went by, it became obvious that John and I couldn't keep the airlines in business forever," Tish
says. "We were scheduled to take a trip to Venice together and I was
very excited to be able to spend some time with John without having
to jump back on a plane on a Monday morning.

"On our second day in Venice, we came back from shopping and I
noticed an orchid on the bed and thought how nice it was of the hotel
to do that for all their guests. Then I saw a big bouquet of red roses in
the corner of the room. Suddenly John was down on one knee asking
me to marry him. I started crying and just kept saying yes over and
over. He'd brought an engagement ring with him and later said he'd
been a nervous wreck because he was afraid he'd lose it.

"We called my parents, his parents and anyone else we could think
of. It was a deliriously happy time."

Frequently couples are on different emotional timetables. Eventually they sync up if the vibe is right. Here's how it went with Pat
and Mark:

"We dated for two years and I was thirty-eight when we got
engaged. It happened in Paris—my favorite city. But Paris almost

didn't happen! I was overseeing a major television project there and we planned to sightsee for a few days beforehand. And in my mind I had a huge romantic fantasy of going to Paris with someone I loved—him. I didn't expect him to propose, but the trip had become a big deal.

"Close to our travel date, we're on the phone, and he says, 'I'm not sure I can go to Paris. Work is very busy.' All my alarm bells went off!

"Now, I was never, ever assertive in a romantic relationship (remember Mr. Unavailable?). But this man and this relationship were different. Most of all, I was different. I knew he was busy, but I also knew he could make it work. I told him, 'If you don't come to Paris with me, I hear what you're saying.' 'I'm just busy,' he said. 'No,' I said, 'it's very important to me that you come, and what I hear you saying is that *our relationship* is not going anywhere.'

"He came. A couple of days before my project started, my heart was set on taking a day trip to see the roses in the beautiful gardens of the painter Claude Monet. Mark was equally set on our taking a dinner cruise in Paris that evening. At the train station we discovered we'd been given the wrong train schedule: if we went to the gardens, we wouldn't be back in time for our dinner cruise.

"I don't cry easily, but I was so disappointed that I cried in the train station. 'All right,' Mark said, 'we'll skip the dinner and just go to the gardens.' That's what we did, and I thought it was one of the best days of my life.

"The next evening, after a romantic dinner, Mark insisted we have champagne at the restaurant perched atop the Eiffel Tower. At the private entrance, the attendant asked if we had a dinner reservation. 'No,' Mark says. Another snag: 'It is required, *monsieur*.' 'That's OK,' I said. 'Let's just go up and enjoy the full moon.'

"So there we are at the top of the Eiffel Tower, and Mark turns to me and blurts out, 'Ryan (as he calls me), will you marry me?'

"Apparently, after that predeparture conversation, Mark was worried I might call it quits, and he was planning to propose—first on the dinner cruise and then over champagne at the Eiffel Tower—but his plans kept going awry. Standing there among all the tourists, I started crying (now from happiness) and said, 'Oh, I'd love to.'

"We still joke about it: I wanted to marry Mark so badly and I could have been engaged two days earlier if I hadn't burst into tears in the train station! But in the end I had it all: the roses, a full moon over Paris and a proposal from my go-to guy, who finds a way to make things work even when his best-laid plans don't. It was one of those unforgettable weeks that you put in your emotional bank and draw on when you need it."

Of all the brides we know, Ann and Irv were the biggest slowpokes to get on the same page engagement-wise. "Although we knew almost from the beginning (within a month for Irv and within a year for me) that we'd always be together, we were both gun-shy about marriage. First he wanted to and I didn't; then I wanted to and he didn't! Although we were constantly together, we kept separate apartments—I wasn't ready to take the big step of moving in together.

"One summer Irv was talking about buying a house. I was ready to marry, but he hadn't proposed. I told him the house decision was his. The message was clear: *It's your house, not ours.*

"One evening after a phone call from the real estate agent, he said to me, 'I'm not going to buy a house. But I want to marry you.' I said, 'Are you sure you want to do this?' We just couldn't seem to get it together!

"The next night, as we were sitting on the couch, he suddenly got down on one knee and said, 'Would you do me the honor of being my wife?' Well, of course I would! After ten years of hesitations about being married, finally it just seemed silly not to be. We were thrilled when we finally tied the knot. So were our friends and families: at our wedding when I welcomed our guests, I said, 'I know some of you are as surprised as we are to be here,' and everyone laughed!"

It's natural to be nervous about taking this big step. Talk it through together and be patient with each other. It's all part of combining complex lives.

WHY THEY WED

"Getting married was honoring our relationship. When we did, suddenly everything was different. No longer was it 'his' and 'mine'; it was 'ours.'"

"We didn't have children and didn't plan to, but I really believe in marriage. I enjoy being married. I feel more secure being married. And I love having a partner in everything."

"There was no real reason for us to get married, but now that we are, we're so much more of a couple: he has my back and I have his. We are totally a team."

"When we met with the minister, he suddenly turned to Matthew and said, 'Why are you getting married again?' Matt said without missing a beat, 'Because I can't imagine life without her. I want to protect her and support her.'"

What's an appropriate length of time for an engagement?

What's appropriate is whatever works for your man and you. One bride insisted on a yearlong engagement. It had been a long-distance relationship, and her previous marriage had wounded her emotionally and financially. She needed time to feel sure of this new love. But another bride, also remarrying, laughed about her whirlwind engagement: "When I called the caterer in June for an August date, he thought it was a shotgun wedding!" Tish, too, was ready to marry after John popped the question: "We got engaged in May and married in October. I think long engagements give couples too much time to obsess. I'd say to older brides, 'Figure out who you want in your wedding party and where you want it to be, order your invitations and do it!'"

If you feel sure you've found the right mate, your engagement will be a whirlwind time of joyful anticipation. One bride put it well: "Once the planning starts, there's no time to keep thinking about whether you've made the right choice. I was continually aware during the planning that my fiancé was the only element of the wedding that I was absolutely sure about, and what a good thing that was!"

Sharing Your Joy

We each have a large circle of friends, family and coworkers. How should we go about telling everyone?

Sharing news of your engagement enhances your happiness by spreading it to the world. Most people start with family (especially their children), then friends, then coworkers.

GET THE WORD OUT!

Make sure the gossip mill doesn't inform intimates before you do!

Some single friends may need a little time to adjust to your good tidings. One bride recalls, "My oldest friend sounded sort of shocked and got off the phone quickly. We'd gone through many relationship ups and downs together, and she didn't have a man in her life at the moment. She couldn't have been happier for me later; she just had to get used to the idea."

A single girlfriend's happiness for you may be bittersweet: she wants to meet someone she's crazy about, too. You've been there, so you can understand how she feels. One bride told us, "It was difficult to announce my engagement to my singles group, but when I wore my engagement ring to a holiday party, someone noticed it. They were all so supportive and later threw me a surprise shower. I did console one woman who became emotional during the shower, telling me, 'I want what you have.' Of course, I wanted her to have her heart's desire as well." We want that, too—that's why we wrote this book!

Often our girlfriends, who know us better than anyone, are the first to spot a likely match. Lisa met Anton at a January party she attended with several girlfriends. On Valentine's Day her pals secretly wrote down their prediction that the two would wed. Nine months later, they read it at her wedding!

TELLING THE EX

Whether to tell the ex depends on your situation. If children are involved and in contact with the ex, clearly the ex will need to know. But before you do anything, and even if you get along with the ex, check with your attorney first to review your divorce and custody agreements. You want to make sure you fully understand and are following its terms and stipulations.

continued

continued from last page

Even if children aren't involved, there are times when notifying the ex is the respectful thing to do, particularly if the ex lives in your community or nearby and might learn of your nuptials via newspaper announcement, church bulletin or overlapping social circles, or if you might be seen with your fiancé at public functions. One woman simply contacted her ex-husband and said, "I didn't want you to hear from someone else that I'm getting married in the next month or so."

We've started planning our wedding and bringing our families into the loop. Most are 100 percent happy for us and eager to participate . . . a few not so much. Any advice?

Our brides shared lots of stories about this—many positive, some "not so much"! In grown-up life, not everyone's immediately on board with big changes. You can sympathize with their feelings without agreeing with them: "We had friends who took the red-eye to attend our wedding, but Mack's three grown daughters didn't come, although they live in a city not that far away. Mack insisted they'd change their minds, but I knew better and kept trying to prepare him by saying, 'Honey, don't be disappointed, but they're not coming.' I don't think my husband will ever get over the hurt and embarrassment in front of the rest of his family. I believe the reason the girls didn't show up was from a sense of loyalty to their mother, but it was wrong of them to hurt their father as they did."

It's wise, as this bride noted, not to assume that somehow things will just work themselves out. From brides who faced family challenges realistically and resourcefully, we heard some remarkable turnaround stories.

"When Dennis and I took his parents to dinner and told them we were engaged, his mother literally turned to him and said, 'How could you do this to me?'" Yasmin told us. "I was the 'wrong' background. For months she implored Dennis not to marry me. Finally he told her, 'I'd really like you and Dad to come to our wedding, but if you can't come and behave, then please don't come.' They came, but his mother started to make some comments to me. That's when I said, 'I think you and I need to start fresh, and I don't think my wedding is the appropriate time or place for us to be talking about this. So if you'll excuse me, I have to say good-night to a few of my guests.' And I walked away.

"Afterward, I started over with her. I was unfailingly polite. I sent cards at appropriate times. I phoned. What happened was extraordinary. Nine months after we got married, she hosted a lovely catered brunch to introduce me to her friends. Before the guests arrived, Dennis was very nervous. Finally he said to his mother, 'I don't get it. Why are you doing this?' She turned to him and said, 'I was not very nice to you. So I wanted to do something nice now. I've never seen you so happy.' She turned to me and said, 'I've never heard anyone call him *sweetheart*. How could I not love you?'"

Brooke's mother-in-law disapproved of her because of religious differences and because she was older than her husband. Brooke decided "not to draw a line in the sand. I concentrated on my husband and making his happiness my number one priority. I wanted his mother to see that I loved her only son and that nothing was more important to me. It was a lot for her to accept, but I just kept focusing on my husband and also on being good to her. I made sure she and my husband spent time alone together. I often suggest to him that he take her to lunch without me. We've been married for three years and she has come around. She sees how happy I've made her son."

Tatiana told us, "My older sister and I are very close, and as my honor attendant she was supposed to help me out, but something always seemed to come up if I needed her assistance with reception planning or invitations, or just as a sounding board. It was as if my finally getting married meant she couldn't be my big sister anymore. In a few months things were fine, and I was glad I hadn't confronted her. If I'd been younger, I would have kept trying to draw her in. As an older bride, I was disappointed but more than capable of carrying on by myself with the help of my fabulous friends. Besides, I was so happy that nothing could dim the day. I was doing everything I wanted for *me*—that was the most important thing."

These women handled family challenges without letting them dim their happiness, from their wedding day forward. As Yasmin said, "I felt so loved and surrounded by good feelings at my wedding that it didn't touch me that day." In the end, their positive approach benefited everyone. Never underestimate the power of happiness and love to transform relationships.

Many brides told us of poignant, memorable family celebrations. Ann recalls, "When Irv and I got engaged, he wanted to tell his grown son and daughter first, and in person. We took them out to dinner, and he said something adorably exaggerated like, 'Well, kids, I want to tell you that after all this time, Ann has finally agreed to marry me.' They were thrilled for us and bought us a drink to celebrate. It was intimate and sweet and fun."

"My husband's son wasn't able to attend our wedding," said one bride, a widow who remarried in her seventies, "so a month before we married, we flew to Chicago, where he and his wife held a party for us at his club. He wrote a poem about finding love later in life and had dozens of red roses delivered to the club. Every woman who came in that night received a rose and a copy of the poem. After dinner we went downstairs for a drink at the bar, and all the patrons congratulated us. It was a wonderful evening and we were both truly touched."

You and your man have finally found each other. Let your joy shine through, and it will be contagious.

The Big Picture: You Paint It

We're getting a lot of advice about what's "appropriate" for our wedding. Is there a "right" way to do this?

What's right for you is *your* call. Some brides have cherished wedding dreams for years. Others are nuptial novices: "I never doodled bridal outfits in my notebook. And my mother never mentioned the subject once!" (Not everyone we interviewed had moms who kept mum. One bride laughed: "My mother planned my first wedding—including picking the groom!")

If you're younger and your parents are paying for your wedding, you tend to go along with what they want and don't give yourself a chance to think about doing something a little different. As a mature bride, chances are you and your honey are paying for the wedding (maybe with a bit of help), and you can make any wedding dream you have come true.

Tish says, "If I'd gotten married in my twenties, I'm sure my parents would have paid for the wedding, but we paid for this wedding ourselves. That made things simple: basically, there were only two people who needed to agree on the details, and we could invite our parents to enjoy the day as our guests."

Whether it's your first wedding or your third, and whether you're thirty-five or sixty-five, being a grown-up means *you* get to make the decisions. Throw a bash if you want. Elope if you prefer! We know a bride who looked at twenty-two reception sites and one who got flowers from a vendor in the park en route to her ceremony. We know brides who wore white, wore green, wore purple, wore pants. Do anything you want!

THE ONLY RULE ABOUT WEDDINGS

The only "rule" is that your wedding reflect you and your man. As Ann says, "This is a celebration. Do what you'd do to celebrate in the way both of you want. I think a lot of people feel, 'I'm too old for that.' You're not. You should feel terrific about it, and you should do whatever you want."

One bride who married for the first time at fifty-five to a man nine years her senior told us, "I agonized for months before deciding that at our stage of life a wedding with no fuss, some close friends and sandwiches and punch in the back garden was about right. Either that or we should elope. Then Jeremy asked me why I wanted to be married. My answer—to make public our love and celebrate it in front of our friends and loved ones! So elopement didn't really fit the bill. Jeremy was reminding me that I should do whatever I wanted, since it was my one and only wedding." The Garter Brides agree!

Another bride refused to let her age—eighty!—rhyme with sedately. She and her husband held their wedding and celebratory dinner at a restaurant they loved . . . and just kept inviting people to join the fun: "When we got to the capacity of the restaurant," she said, "we stopped!" This is one time when we *don't* advise grown-up brides to act their age!

But you *can* apply your grown-up ingenuity to logistics and budgeting decisions: "I refused to buy into all the nonsense younger brides get sucked into," Kate told us. "When I realized how much it was going to cost to have my wedding at a club, I decided my 'fifteen minutes of fame' weren't worth it. My parents offered to host a small wedding at their apartment and gave us the money they would have spent on a bigger wedding. We used the money to do some renovations on our apartment."

WORDS TO THE WISE ON WEDDINGS

"Don't let anyone rain on your parade. If you want a big, flashy wedding—do it! If you want small and intimate—do it! You deserve whatever your heart has always desired. Don't be too practical; be the bride you always dreamed of being, surrounded by the people you love and who love you—and enjoy yourself."

"Make your wedding your dream come true. Don't get caught up in what others have done. It's *your* wedding, *your* dream. Just have fun!"

"One of my girlfriends told me, 'No matter how carefully you plan a wedding, *something* will go wrong, but just laugh about it.' I give this advice now to all my friends because it was true for me!"

"When we met with the rabbi before we married, he said, 'This is a wonderful time, but also a stressful time. There's so much to consider.' He was so wise and comforting. He made us feel that it was OK to be nervous, even while feeling incredibly happy."

A Cast of Thousands? Involving Friends and Family in Your Wedding

We're touched and humbled by how many people have offered to help us. What can they do?

Lots! You and your fiancé have nurtured many relationships over the years, and now all of these talented folks can help make your wedding unforgettable, whether by their presence as guests or as members of the wedding party, with their participation in the preparations or by putting their abilities to work in ways you may never have anticipated!

Many brides shared funny, rapturous and touching stories of how friends and family pulled out the stops to be there for them. "The speeches our friends and family gave at our wedding were hysterical. My wildly successful brother flew in from Paris and brought the house down with childhood reminiscences about his older sister and how his lifelong inferiority complex was all my fault! I could do nothing but cry and laugh, since brides are not supposed to retaliate during their wedding! The best man arrived from Rome to say fascinating things about the groom, whom he has known since college, and one of my cousins showed up from South Carolina with an equally wicked speech recollecting my childhood."

Friends, Indeed!

Your long, strong friendships offer great opportunities to give your girlfriends special roles. As bridesmaids and honor attendants, they can celebrate with you (in one case we know of, a friend officiated) and be your closest advisers—or, as one bride fondly called them, "my bridal cabinet."

Another bride, planning bicoastal receptions, built a team from her far-flung friends: "My East Coast friends visited sites and tested the food; a West Coast friend looked at sites she could get to more easily than I."

Pat, who loves to cook for and with her friends (she baked wedding cakes for several Garter Brides, including Ann), said, "I'd been in fourteen weddings and didn't want anyone to have to buy a dress for mine, so other than my mother as my honor attendant, I didn't have a wedding party. Instead, some of my closest local girlfriends and I made special cookies to pass around at the reception."

There's nothing like a girlfriend to settle bridal nerves. "On the day of the wedding, I felt like a teenager. I was nervous, silly, running late, under-organized and not at all in control!" Ann describes one friend's wise remedy for bridal jitters: "A dear friend called and said, 'Ann, the week before the wedding, I will be absolutely available to you. Say the word and I'll be there'"—and she lived in Washington, D.C.! She even offered to come over the day of the wedding to help me get dressed. Even though I wasn't nervous, I don't know what I'd have done without her. When Pat got married, I did the same for her, including coming early on her wedding day to help her get ready, bringing extra panty-hose, needle and thread, safety pins and other emergency supplies— including a new lipstick and Tampax!"

Another bride's best friend spontaneously greeted her at the reception with a refreshing drink and then whisked her off to the ladies' room, where she got a few precious minutes to sit and relax while her friend produced a comb and hairpins from her purse and fixed the bride's hair, which had become mussed from receiving line hugs. "How did you know I needed this?" the bride marveled. "I'm married!" her friend reminded her.

"When Irv and I set our wedding date, I was very disappointed that two of my oldest friends couldn't attend due to important family obligations," Ann recalls. "My dear friend Jackie (from seventh grade) sent me her beautiful white beaded evening bag to carry, and Barbara loaned me her pearl earrings. Even though I couldn't have them with me, they could still be part of that special day by providing two wonderful items for 'something borrowed'!"

Meaningful Roles for Family

The diversity of grown-up families allows multiple generations to participate in your nuptials. Adult children can offer tender, insightful reminiscences. One bride told us, "My husband's younger son, who had aided and abetted our blossoming romance, made a speech full of the kind of sweet, intimate details only a family member would know about." Ann recalls, "Irv's son was his best man and gave us a wonderful toast. Irv had his own and Tony's names engraved on his father's pocketwatch (which had his father's name already engraved on it) and gave it to Tony as a groom's gift."

Tish's wedding party was tiny—in both size and stature: "John's daughter and son, ages seven and five, stood up with us. His daughter was beautiful in a flowing pink dress and his son was adorable in a little white tux. When I was planning our wedding, knowing that I would soon become a stepmom, it was very important to me to include John's children in the wedding party. I honestly couldn't decide which of my girlfriends to ask to be bridesmaids, so we decided to have John's two kids be our entire wedding party.

"Of course, I had to have my hair and my stepdaughter's hair done on the big day . . . and it took forever! John got to the church with my brothers with the idea of meeting us early to make sure the kids were set for the ceremony. As the minutes dragged by, he became convinced I wasn't going to show up. When we finally walked in, I don't think he'd ever been so glad to see anyone in his life!

"Having kids in our wedding was fun because we could make plans with them and choose their outfits together, and it gave us all a focus for the weeks before the event. We let them invite a few friends so they weren't the only kids at the reception. Having them standing up there with us showed all our guests that we were now a new family—the four of us—moving forward."

Young girls will cherish the chance to dress up and participate, so don't stop at one flower girl if you don't want to. "We had four flower girls, all nine years old: his two nieces, my niece and a close friend's daughter."

One bride enriched her garden wedding with a variant on the flower girl theme: "Our five-year-old 'butterfly maiden' managed to read the Native American butterfly legend—that butterflies carry wishes and dreams into the universe—all by herself with some help from my brother. Then we released monarch butterflies into the garden, which was designed for butterflies to enjoy, to a chorus of oohs and ahhs and applause."

WHY THEY WED

"I had found my true love at last."

"I married to preserve and cherish what we already had together. So when people ask, 'How's married life?' I say, 'Just as wonderful as it was before.'"

"My father used to ask, 'So, when are you going to find somebody?' I was never in a rush and would shrug him off. When he met Arturo for the first time, I looked at my dad and said, 'This was worth waiting for, Dad.'"

"When I was married the first time, I was a kid. The second time I had a much different personality and I was ready for a partnership. This time there's no pressure to have children or find a career; you do it just because you want to be with him."

Children can be included in vows. "I took vows to Ken's son, Evan, after we said our own vows. There wasn't a dry eye in the house!" one bride told us.

Even departed loved ones or those who can't attend can be honored and included: "Neither my husband nor I have living parents, so we set up a table in the ceremony area to hold their photographs and have them present in this evocative sense." One bride added a twenty-first-century twist: her parents, who lived in another city, were too elderly to attend, but she called them on her cell phone so they could hear the small, private ceremony!

Some people are asking "which marriage" this is for my fiancé and me . . . why I'm wearing white "at my age" . . . and even about our financial arrangements. What should I say?

Weddings are exciting! Everyone wants to get in on the act. Although their inquiries are mostly well-meant, the spectrum of inappropriateness can range from the moderately annoying to the *"What?"*

For questions about finances, try a confident "We've got everything worked out" with no details offered. If someone asks why you're wearing white, counter with, "Why not?" For questions about remarriage, we think Pat's husband got it right: "When someone asked Mark which marriage this was for him, he said, 'My last.'"

A FUNNY THING HAPPENED . . .

"This 'mature bride' at a youthful fifty-one was somehow presumed to be the mother of the bride while dress hunting, registering and selecting wedding items: 'What kind of kitchenware has the bride chosen?' 'The bride is choosing the kitchenware as we speak. *Hmph.*' The upside of my (alleged) maturity, however, was in being able to keep in perspective the pressure and the number of decisions to be made. None of that was as important as having found exactly the right partner at last. The rest would work itself out, and it did."

Let's Party!

My friends want to give me a bridal shower, and some people have asked if we're registered. Is it OK to do both? What about other kinds of parties?

"If anyone offers to throw you a shower," one bride advised, "say yes."

It's OK to have a bridal shower if you've been married before, and certainly if you've never been. These days, the number and nature of parties before (and after) the big day need only be limited by your imagination. From traditional kitchen and lingerie showers with hors d'oeuvres, coffee, wine and games to restaurant dinners with friends to coed showers that include your fiancé, the brides we interviewed described myriad celebrations that added to the fun of their nuptials:

- "My future sisters-in-law threw a shower for about ten of my close friends. I still have the baseball cap with a white veil that says 'bride,' and my husband still has his 'groom' baseball cap—not to mention the lingerie!"

- "We had a party with a belly dancer."

- "A group of friends took me out to dinner—sans sexy underwear and naked men clambering out of cakes. I loved it."

- "The night before our wedding, we had a pool party and barbecue at our house."

- "My women friends gave me a shower where I requested 'words of wisdom' as a gift."

- "I had an engagement party and five showers, given by joyous friends and my sister, a rehearsal dinner and an impromptu postwedding gathering for wedding leftovers in our hotel room with about ten friends who were staying in the hotel overnight."

- "We had a prewedding dinner the night before for the huge number of out-of-town guests. It wasn't so good for my middle-age wrinkles, but they had come a long way and needed to be welcomed."

As for gifts and registering, Ann says, "It was my third marriage and Irv's second, and I considered not having gifts. But a friend who'd gotten married for the second time at around fifty said, 'Ann, let people give you wedding presents. You're starting a life together, and you should treat it that way. That's why you register.'"

HOW THEY WED

- "We were married in a church in a little seaside town, followed by a reception in a Federalist-style brick building, with tall windows, a gold chandelier and hardwood floors. Very New England."

- "Our wedding included Chinese traditions—my daughter is Chinese and we felt that would be a way to honor and include her—and my daughter and my husband's son were our only witnesses."

- "One of my favorite things was our decision to include everyone in the wedding readings. The audience was asked to acknowledge that they had a responsibility to us as our 'community'—that it takes a village to make a marriage work."

- "Our friends decorated a 1963 Edsel pickup truck (we called it the 'mitzvah/chuppah-mobile') and they led us in a procession, playing the bagpipes in Scottish kilts and tartan yarmulkes, down a country road to the courtyard of the inn where we married."

continued

continued from last page

- "We were married outdoors at a nature preserve."

- "We were married in the main sanctuary of my temple with only the immediate family (about eighteen people) present. Afterward we went to a nearby club for drinks and were serenaded by the rabbi, who is a classical pianist. Then we went to a quiet, romantic restaurant for dinner *à deux*. A month later we held a dinner for a hundred friends at a club."

- "I created a very intimate wedding in my sister's backyard. There were twelve of us plus the rabbi."

- "We married in the garden of a Greek restaurant, with a Latin jazz group playing our music, and all our friends pronounced us husband and wife."

- "My second wedding was a traditional Catholic mass."

- "I was married in a small Greek Orthodox church. We were supposed to have about 125 guests, but honestly I'm not sure how many were there, since it was a buffet brunch with open seating and my mother kept inviting people!"

- "We had two weddings: one in a Catholic church, followed by a Jewish service at a lovely hotel. We wanted to respect each of our religious backgrounds without making our wedding a hybrid that didn't reflect our religious practices."

- "We had a priest and a rabbi jointly bless us in Hebrew and English."

Vows That Wow

Every moment of your wedding ceremony—the words, the music and the mystical magic—can and should reflect the essence of you and your mate.

Tish and John made beautiful music together at their wedding, just as they had in high school: "We got married in New York City in a church on Madison Avenue before taking a horse-drawn carriage to our reception at the Boathouse in Central Park. During the ceremony, we sang 'Let It Be Me' to each other, singing the third verse in harmony. We wanted to hold hands, but in rehearsal, we both got so emotional we knew we'd never get through it, so we didn't touch each other." (P.S.: when they renewed their vows for their fifteenth anniversary, they sang it again.)

"We mingled faiths and friends at our wedding," Pat recalls. "The chuppah was held by two other interfaith couples who were close friends and was embroidered with the names of all the couples married under it. The priest who blessed our rings was a dear friend who often dropped by my apartment to talk after his power walks around the neighborhood. At our ceremony he told how when he'd leave, I'd say, 'Father, say a prayer that I'll meet someone special.' 'One day,' he said, 'I went to Pat's apartment and when she opened the door she said, "So you've been praying."'"

Ann went traditional for nuptials number three: "A lot of women I know who've gotten married later in life said they felt self-conscious about having a traditional wedding. We decided we weren't going to. We had a very conventional ceremony in an upstairs room at a club, attended by just the immediate family. One of the most beautiful moments was when the rabbi wrapped us in the prayer shawl. Afterward, there was dinner and dancing for about ninety-five guests in the ballroom with an excellent three-piece band."

Another couple tipped the opposite end of the formality scale: "We left our apartment, got flowers and walked to Central Park, where we got married in a gazebo on the lake. Aside from our two witnesses and the minister, we had just two guests: one who took pictures and one who was only two years old! We also had two surprise guests: it was raining lightly and two teenagers taking refuge in the gazebo became our 'extra witnesses.' It was spontaneous, simple and perfect."

SOME FUNNY THINGS HAPPENED . . .

"When Irv's elderly uncle left our wedding, I said, 'Thank you so much for coming.' Everyone laughed when he replied, 'Thank *you* for taking him off our hands!'"

"We were married in my in-laws' living room. They had two miniature schnauzers who somehow sensed the importance of the day: when we entered the living room where the guests were assembled, the dogs followed in formation behind us! Everyone broke out in laughter."

"I tracked the weather for weeks before our outdoor wedding. All looked good until a hurricane started creating havoc out at sea. It poured during the ceremony, and although we were under a tent, so much rain had gathered on the tent roof that at a very tender moment in the ceremony, the minister, who was standing at the edge of the tent, had a bucketful of water fall on his head! He made the best of it and we carried on."

"My seven-year-old son asked his father (my ex) during the ceremony to give me a kiss because I was crying!"

Many of the brides imbued their ceremonies with creative touches reflecting a lifetime of experiences, talents and interests: "We were married under an azure sky in a friend's garden that my husband had designed and landscaped. A Buddhist priest officiated in a ceremony of our own devising in which we told each other why we had selected each other as life partners. The priest cleansed our rings in a purification ritual. At the end, the strains of 'Scotland the Brave' wafted from the back of the property. A lone bagpiper emerged through the trees and played until lunch was served. My husband was astonished—I had surprised him with the music of his ancestors."

MORE WORDS TO THE WISE ON WEDDINGS

"Other brides assured me *something* would go wrong right before the wedding. Sure enough, the caterer called to ask if I was aware that the beautiful mansion where we were to wed was encased in scaffolding, with Dumpsters and sand piles out front. Why no, I wasn't! We worked it out: sand and Dumpsters were removed, the scaffolding stayed but was removed from the door and the price was reduced accordingly. The trick was in appearing to be horrified and overwhelmed to get the immediate cooperation I needed, while staying calm internally. Advice to brides: stay cool in the face of apparent disaster. It *will* all work out. After thirty years of being single, nothing could ruin my having found my soul mate!"

"I wish I'd had my hair done professionally—I didn't calculate on breezes and open air. But my toenails and fingernails looked fine!"

"I was so overwhelmed by all the funny and touching speeches that I forgot my thank-you list and regret that I hadn't prepared better. I forgot to acknowledge my husband's children—something I'll always regret."

"During the ceremony, look around at your guests and really try to take everything in."

"At the eleventh hour I decided to have the event videotaped—solely because my favorite elderly aunt, who couldn't attend, said, 'You can always send me a videotape, dear!' Now I'm so grateful I did, as everything went by in a misty blur. We both wept when we watched the tape later; it was so moving. Whether you hire someone or have friends take photos and videos, make sure you have a record of the day."

Destination weddings let you take your big day anywhere in the world that inspires you: "We had a small ceremony on an island in Alaska called Halibut Cove, with twenty-four guests, mainly family and close friends. We all took a little fishing boat to the island and I was married on a wooden dock overlooking the most beautiful scenery I've ever seen. After a dinner of clams and mussels at the only restaurant in the cove, we took the boat home at midnight, with the sun just setting on an Alaskan summer night. Perfection!"

Perfect Reception

Our heads are spinning with ideas for the reception! Any advice?

Hitch up your skirts, cuffs, kilts or what-have-you and kick up your heels! Just listening to our brides talk about their receptions made us want to shimmy! Whether they feasted on filet mignon and smoked salmon (that was Pat's) or filched candy from fishbowls set out for the twenty-plus kids in attendance, sipped Bellinis or swigged beer, fox-trotted or square-danced, their parties were delicious, fun, fanciful, sophisticated, sassy and even endearingly silly—in short, as varied as the couples themselves—and that's our advice to you as you plan your festivities! We want you to be able to say, as one bride did: "I must have been glowing—never have pictures of me looked so good." Read on for highlights of the fêtes, the food, the cake, the clothes and, at the center of each, a beautiful bride with the man of her dreams.

How They Celebrated

- "We had champagne, caviar, dinner and cake. It was lovely."
- "We had a blowout party in a cathedral that we turned into a nightclub."

- "During dinner, my husband's best friend (and master of ceremonies) got up and said, 'There are some people outside who you didn't invite, but they decided to come anyway.' In marched a fifteen-piece bagpipe band in full regalia playing 'Hava Nagila' and a group of guys lifted our chairs and danced us around the room. The band then presented him with a token of their affection—a tartan yarmulke!"

- "We had a sit-down lunch for fifty, a lousy photographer, a great wedding cake, fabulous food and a crazy karaoke guy. Cake and coffee were served in the billiards room, where you could shoot pool or sing with the karaoke guy, who made people wear costumes. The best was the group of guys, including my husband, who dressed as Village People and sang 'YMCA.' It was such a hit my husband's dad joined in and danced around with an inflatable cake hat on his head!"

- "We had yummy passed hors d'oeuvres, followed by a buffet with informal café seating. Not only was it less expensive than a sit-down dinner, but I didn't have to do a seating plan, worrying where to seat people who didn't get along or might not have much in common. We just mingled and had fun—me included!"

- "We wanted something low-key and booked a restaurant we liked, which closed for us and our sixty guests. We were married there by an interfaith rabbi, and we had a string and flute trio and a sit-down lunch. My husband's parents couldn't understand how we could consider it a wedding without a band and dancing. Shortly after the wedding his mother invited us to their home to meet some of their friends. We were surprised to arrive and find over two hundred guests! All I did was stand on a receiving line shaking hands with people, 90 percent of whom I never saw again. My in-laws refer to it as our 'wedding reception,' but we had the wedding and party we wanted. Had I been in my twenties, I probably would have agreed to the big blowout they wanted."

- "We've been married fifteen years, but to this day people tell me how much fun they had at our wedding. The morning service was followed by a full brunch with open bar at a wonderful Italian restaurant owned by a friend, with a terrific Greek American band. The Old World ambiance and merriment were just what I wanted."

LET THEM EAT CAKE

Pat remembers, "I bake wedding cakes as a hobby, so I baked my own: chocolate with raspberry filling—a recipe from a cookbook Mark and I bought in London."

Jenn says, "My wedding cake was the most beautiful I'd ever seen: a lemon cake with pale yellow butter cream icing, decorated with flowers matching my bouquet. The fact that my good friend Patricia Mary Agnes Ryan Lampl baked it made it incredibly special."

"We had two wonderful black-and-white wedding cakes, in tilted, patterned triple tiers—one for our West Coast ceremony and one for our East Coast ceremony."

"Ours was a fruit-tart-like Venetian wedding cake."

"Instead of a traditional wedding cake, my fiancé, his sons and I went to a favorite restaurant and picked four cakes to serve."

Tish laughs. "I told the caterer I wanted a chocolate wedding cake, but to make sure no one put rum in it because we had a lot of little kids at our wedding. Of course, John and I cut into the cake, took a bite and found it *soaked* in rum—but by then it was too late: the pieces were cut and the kids were eating them before we even turned around! They all survived and had a *really* good time, and we still laugh about it!"

What They Wore

Remember Ann wore white? "I didn't know what to wear, so I called a costume designer and said, 'I don't want to look like another guest at the party, but I'm no ingénue.' She suggested a store that sells antique wedding dresses. I fell in love with a delicate, long, cream-colored 1906 Edwardian cotton dress. I felt fantastic in it."

Pat, who claims all her childhood fantasies were "connected with food, Hollywood or both," said, "My fantasy from age fifteen was to wear the dress Grace Kelly wore in *Rear Window* to bring James Stewart the lobster dinner. I didn't have much money to spend. I went to a bridesmaid dress store that sold cocktail dresses and ordered it in ivory: very 1950s with a sweetheart neckline, nipped-in waist and calf-length pouf skirt. And great Peter Fox shoes—on sale—that I still wear."

Tish, bless her performer's heart, went backless! "My brother came over to say hi—and when I turned around, he gasped."

Said another gutsy bride: "It was a very New York wedding: we both wore black. So did our minister—black leather!"

Nita and her groom both wore pants: "We both wore suits, he with a traditional shirt and tie, me with a camisole. For the reception, I wore a long claret spaghetti-strap dress with a shimmery shawl."

Daphne went yesteryear in a Victorian-style long gown. "I designed and made a large lace and ostrich feather hat, with a removable back veil. Without the veil, the hat reversed to show the large flower in front. For something old and something blue, I incorporated a piece of the blue veil from my mother's wedding hat of fifty-nine years before."

Here are a few more highlights:

- "For my second wedding I squeezed into my mother's restored wedding dress that ripped every time I moved!"

■ "I wore a mermaid gown decorated with lace and crystals. He wore a tux with a periwinkle blue cummerbund, and my five bridesmaids wore periwinkle blue dresses."

■ "I'm short, so I didn't want anything overwhelming. I wore a white gown with hand-beaded white Belgian lace on the bodice and arms, and the skirt was pure white satin silk. For something old I wore a ring and a bracelet; for something new I wore a garter (also my something blue), a pair of silver and diamond earrings from my sister, lacy undergarments and beaded silver heels. Vince looked so handsome in his black tuxedo—his mother kept telling him to take off his glasses (though he's as blind as a bat without them) whenever we needed to take a picture."

■ "My husband said he loved me in yellow, so I wore a yellow suit. The flowers were all yellow and blue."

■ "I wore an ivory strapless gown with a champagne lace overlay with long sleeves. I loved it."

We'll leave the final word on this to Pat, who said to Mark about her walk down the aisle: "Remember that when you see me, I'll remember for the rest of my life what you say." You'll also remember for the rest of your life how you feel in the outfit of your dreams—which, like your man, should be exactly right for you.

Over the (Honey)moon

After all the festivities, it's time to escape with your man for some one-on-one R&R! Some of our brides went to exotic isles. Tish and John escaped to the Bahamas before returning to plunge into life as a new family with two little ones (and, as we know, two soon to be on the way). Another couple explored Bora Bora and Tahiti. Ann and Irv went to Club Med. Pat and Mark took a cruise. Others sought bright lights and big cities, striking desert landscapes or both: "We were whisked away in a limo for a night in New York before flying to Santa Fe for a glorious and romantic week. And now we are living happily ever after." Ahhhh.

So decide what defines "play" for the two of you . . . and make sure you do it. Don't just go back to work! As Ann says, "I know a lot of people say, 'We don't really need a honeymoon.' You do. You need a few days to yourselves, away from all the activity. It's important to mark the new beginning of your life as a married couple." If money's tight, see if you can use some frequent-traveler miles, or if a friend who lives in a cool place is away on business or vacation, see if you can borrow her home for a few days (and water her plants while you're at it). You can always plan and save for a bigger getaway later, but you only get one honeymoon with your honey, so make sure you take it, and revel in the special afterglow of your wedding.

And Now . . . Wedded Bliss

We hope reading about the many ways our brides got married has inspired you to pursue your own dreams of wedded bliss. As we listened to their stories, we were once again struck by the optimism and dedication with which these couples sought each other out, nurtured their love and sometimes overcame challenges in order to stand together before the world and say, "We do." One woman who'd raised two small children on her own after being widowed finally remarried twenty-three years later to a father of three whose divorce had taken four years. When we asked why she had married again, she said, "We've been through so much together and he is so accepting of my family and considers my children his children. He told me he wanted me to be a part of his life for the rest of his life. Marrying was a testament to our relationship and our love for each other. I've spent much of my life caring for other people.

Now I'm learning to let someone take care of me. I don't think marriage is about finding your soul mate; it's about being willing to go on a journey together. My life is so much richer, and my feelings for my husband constantly deepen. I love him more and more each day."

Their weddings were the culmination of a dream. "It was remarkable to see our closest friends and relatives from around the country, all in one room, and beaming. There was such joy throughout the day, coming from my side of the family and from his. The joy spilled over to each of us from the other's side, for being the source of each other's happiness!"

The joy of your wedding day will be with you always. We know that's true for us. One bride said it well: "Recently my husband left me a phone message to cheer me up during a particularly evil day at work: 'I shall never forget the sight of you in your wedding outfit coming toward me for the ceremony.' Reason enough for a fifty-five-year-old to marry the man she loves!"

That joy, of course, is just the beginning of the sustained happiness you'll build together. "The best thing about being married is illustrated in this story: I came home from a day in which several personal and professional projects I'd been developing had come together all at the same time. I was excited about them all, but I knew they'd be a lot of work and I didn't want them to interfere with my new marriage. My husband listened to all my news and my feelings of being overwhelmed, and said, 'Honey, I'm not going anywhere.' That's the best thing about being married—knowing my husband loves me, wants me to be happy and is not going anywhere."

We love that feeling, too. It's one that grown-ups especially know how to treasure: "To share your life with someone you love is a privilege not to be taken for granted. The sorrows are halved, the joys doubled."

WHAT THEY LOVE MOST ABOUT BEING MARRIED

"I can kiss him anytime I want to!"

"I'm with my true love."

"Being introduced as 'his wife.'"

"It still makes me smile to say the words 'my husband.'"

"I'm not in it by myself anymore."

"Falling asleep in his arms."

"Never feeling lonely because we have each other."

"Building a life with someone I love."

"Being with someone who has my best interests at heart."

"Knowing that I'm going to laugh every day."

"All of the above!"

CHAPTER 8
Happily Ever After Can Happen to You

We think there's one thing in the world that could change your life. It's falling in love!

We wrote this book because we believe that single women and men everywhere deserve to find each other, love each other and build richly satisfying lives together. It happened for us—and at a time in our lives when we least expected it. Age doesn't matter! We've proved love can happen anytime, and we know it can happen for you.

In fact, we believe these are great years to meet the man of your dreams. When some of our brides were in their twenties, they felt they had to change themselves to fit others' (or their own) expectations of what relationships were "supposed" to be like. Marrying later in life, bride after bride shared with us their feelings that they added a new dimension to their full and satisfying lives. No longer bound to convention or others' expectations, they find life and love can be spontaneous and creative. Best of all, a man who loves them just the way they are is at their side.

Sometimes our brides laugh about their wonderful love. Ann remembers when Irv said, "I'm so lucky to have found you. How did this happen?" She responded, "You listened to your mother!"

"After a roller-coaster social life, I finally emerged with the understanding that trust, mutual respect and knowing that your partner will always be there for you are what really count. How close you feel to that person on the pillow next to yours at night is a spiritual experience."

"When I was younger, there always seemed to be a lot of competing . . . what I like now is that my husband and I are each other's biggest cheerleaders."

"In my twenties I had to figure out who I was. Now I'm bringing that fully formed person into a mutually loving and respectful relationship. It would have been impossible to do that earlier in my life."

Sometimes they marvel at it: "To share your life with someone you love is a privilege. It's really a miracle to find your soul mate and I feel extremely lucky. I don't take this for granted."

Sometimes they relish the quirky side of love. Pat laughs. "Every wedding anniversary, I meet Mark at the station in my wedding gown—usually I'm also wearing my gardening clogs! He just shakes his head and says, 'Ryan, you're a piece of work.'"

It's been such a joy for us to meet all the other Garter Brides who shared their stories and insights with us. They've been an inspiration! So, if you're still looking to find that special love, keep your hopes high and your heart open. If you're in love now, keep your mind and heart attuned to yourself and your husband and enjoy every moment. We believe every woman deserves to have a man in her life who will say, as Tish's husband did when she asked him what his favorite place to be was—"I'm happy wherever you are."

We want that kind of happiness for you, too!

START YOUR OWN GARTER BRIDES SISTERHOOD!

On her wedding day, one bride handed her garter to her girlfriend, who gave it to another girlfriend, and a new tradition was born. Now you can do the same thing when you become a Garter Bride. As one bride told us, "Knowing I was a Garter Bride made me feel special and that I was part of a wonderful group of women."

When you start your own Garter Bride tradition, you become part of a sisterhood of supportive women dedicated to sharing the joy of making a huge and happy change in their lives. Whether you're soon to be wed, hoping to wed or happily wed, you can start a Garter Brides sisterhood anytime.

Here's how we do it: When one of the Garter Brides has a friend who is getting married, Ann, Pat or Tish lets all the brides know about the newest woman who's about to wear the garter. We all stay in touch via e-mail and everyone is delighted to know that a new Garter Bride will soon walk down the aisle. Some of the brides then share the news with their single girlfriends to let them know, "It happened for us and it can happen for you." Next, the garter goes into the mail—a nice "something borrowed" for the bride!

You and your girlfriends can begin your own Garter Brides sisterhood in any way that works for you! You can stay in touch by e-mail, by phone or in person. It doesn't matter how you do it—what matters is the deep sense of connection, support, good spirits and fun that make sharing the same garter so special. As one bride says, "I never had a sister, so I'm proud to be part of this very special sisterhood of the Garter Brides."

We'd Love to Hear from You!

Please contact us to share your stories of seeking, finding and marrying Mr. Right, and discover how other brides are making grown-up marriages work for them. We hope you'll visit our website at www.thegarterbrides.com. We can't wait to hear from you!

The Garter Brides,
Ann, Pat and Tish

INDEX

ABOUT THE AUTHORS

Ann Blumenthal Jacobs is a story editor and award-winning television producer. She has worked in every aspect of television production, from classical music to hockey. Ann and Pat Lampl are partners in On the Aisle Productions, a media consulting firm. Ann met her husband on a blind date set up by his mother. When she got married, she became a stepmother to two twenty-somethings. Ann is currently studying music history at Juilliard and is an active supporter of Primary Stages' Arts Education Program.

Patricia Ryan Lampl is a magazine columnist, author and an award-winning television producer. She met her husband on a blind date and became a first-time mom and a stepgrandmother all in the same year—at the age of forty-four! Pat is the author of four books for children and, with Ann Jacobs, is a partner in On the Aisle Productions. Pat and Mark can't believe they've been married for seventeen years—time flies when you're having fun!

Tish Rabe is a best-selling children's book author, singer and Emmy-nominated songwriter. She met John Rabe when she was sixteen and they starred together in their high school musical. Years later they ran into each other again and Tish became a first-time bride at thirty-six. She also became an instant stepmom, and she and John had two children together. They've been happily married for twenty-four years and recently welcomed their first grandchild.